THE REDEEMER'S TEARS

THE REDEEMER'S TEARS

WEPT OVER LOST SOULS

A TREATISE ON LUKE 19:41,42

JOHN HOWE

SOLID GROUND CHRISTIAN BOOKS
BIRMINGHAM, ALABAMA USA

Solid Ground Christian Books
2090 Columbiana Rd, Suite 2000
Birmingham, AL 35216
205-443-0311
sgcb@charter.net
http://solid-ground-books.com

The Redeemer's Tears
WEPT OVER LOST SOULS

John Howe (1630-1705)

Taken from 1846 edition by Wiley & Putnam, NY

Solid Ground Classic Reprints

First printing of new edition September 2005

Cover work by Borgo Design, Tuscaloosa, AL
Contact them at nelbrown@comcast.net

Cover painting is entitled *"Die Zerstörung des Tempels von Jerusalem" by* Francesco Hayez (1791-1882). This image has been selected because it pictures the very scene our Lord had before his minds-eye as he wept over Jerusalem in Luke 19:41,42.

ISBN: 1-59925-013-6

Biographical Sketch of John Howe

John Howe was born on May 17, 1630, in Loughborough, Leicestershire. His father was a minister with Puritan sympathies, who, in 1634, was suspended from the ministry by the High Commission Court for praying publicly "that God would preserve the prince in the true religion, of which there was cause to fear" that such would not be the case and that "the young prince might not be brought up in popery." The Howes fled to Ireland in 1635, lived there through the Irish rebellion of 1641, then returned to England in the early 1640s to settle in Lancashire.

Howe earned a bachelor's degree in 1648 at Christ's College, Cambridge. He was influenced there by Henry More and Ralph Cudworth, who were Cambridge Platonists. Howe then went to Brasenose College, Oxford, where he earned a master's degree in 1652. That year he was also elected a fellow at Magdalen College, where Thomas Goodwin was president. He became a member of the Congregational church that Goodwin pastored. During those years, he outlined a book of divinity for his private use, and deviated little from its emphases throughout his life.

At the age of twenty-three, Howe returned to Lancashire. He was ordained there by Charles Herle, the rector of Winwick who had embraced Presbyterian convictions. The next year Howe was asked to be minister of the parish church of Great Torrington, Devonshire. He joined a ministerial fraternal there and became close friends with George Hughes of Plymouth, a minister known for his piety and learning. Howe maintained weekly correspondence in Latin with Hughes; he also met Hughes's daughter Catherine, and married her a year later. They were blessed with four sons and a daughter.

When the Puritans held fast days, Howe worshiped with his flock from 9 A.M. to 4 P.M. He began with a fifteen-minute prayer, then spent forty-five minutes reading and expounding Scripture. After that, he prayed for an hour, preached for an hour, and prayed for half an hour. After a half-hour break, he prayed and preached for another three hours.

In 1656, Oliver Cromwell asked Howe to be one of his chaplains. Howe undertook that task with a profound understanding of the prophetic responsibilities of his ministry. For example, on March 12, 1657, he wrote to Richard Baxter, "I should be exceeding desirous to hear from you, what you understand to be the main evils of the nation that you judge capable of redress by the present government? What [do] you conceive one in my station obliged to urge upon them as matter of duty?"

Howe was a great peacemaker. He did everything he could to reconcile the Presbyterians and the Congregationalists. Yet he did not fear to speak out against wrongdoers, including Cromwell. After one particularly pointed sermon, someone told Howe that he feared Howe might have irrecoverably lost Cromwell's favor. Howe replied, "I have discharged my duty, and will trust the issue with God." Cromwell worked through his resentment, and Howe remained with him until Cromwell died in 1658.

Cromwell's son, Richard, could not successfully fill his father's place. For eighteen months after Cromwell's death, one crisis followed upon another. Richard eventually resigned, and the Presbyterians joined Monk's army in inviting Charles II to return. A brokenhearted Howe wrote to Baxter, "Religion is lost out of England, further than it can creep into corners.... I am returning to my old station, being now at liberty beyond dispute."

Howe returned to his former pastorate at Torrington until the Act of Uniformity passed in 1662. Then he left his congregation, saying, "I have consulted my conscience, and cannot be satisfied with the terms of conformity settled by law." In 1665, he took the oath of passive obedience prescribed by the Five Mile Act. For several years he continued to preach in private houses. Life was difficult for him, as it was for many Nonconformists. Howe wrote, "Many of them live upon charity, some of them with difficulty getting their bread." Unable to preach publicly, Howe prepared for publication sermons he had preached at Torrington. In 1668, he published *The Blessedness of the Righteous*.

In 1671, Lord Massereene of Antrim Castle invited Howe to become his chaplain in Ireland. On the journey to Ireland, high winds drove the ship off course to Holyhead. Having reached land, Howe received an unusual invitation from a stranger on horseback to preach the next Sunday. He preached two times that Sabbath. The ship could not sail the next week because of high winds. A much larger crowd gathered the following Sunday to hear Howe, but Howe was sick in bed. The local minister was so astonished to see so many people that he immediately sent for Howe, who got out of bed and went to preach two more sermons. He preached without notes—as a dying man to dying men. Howe later said, "If my ministry was ever of any use, it must have been then."

Howe found the Irish church less hostile to Nonconformists than the English church. Bishop Down gave him permission to preach in any of the parish churches of his diocese. The Presbyterian ministers valued Howe's presence so highly that he was asked to help preside over their theological seminary.

In 1674, Howe published *Delighting in God*, written from notes of sermons preached at Torrington twenty years before. Two years later, he published the first part of *The Living Temple,* which would become his best-known book.

In 1676, Howe accepted a call to the Silver Street Presbyterian church in London. At first, all went well. He preached to large numbers of people and was esteemed by both Anglicans and Dissenters. Gradually, however, persecution of the Dissenters intensified. In 1683, when the bishop of Lincoln wrote a pastoral letter urging that penal laws against Dissenters be activated, Howe protested.

By 1685, Howe's life was in such danger that he could not walk openly in the streets of London. His health suffered. The ascent of James II to the throne promised even worse things, so Howe accepted an invitation from Philip, Lord Wharton, to tour Europe with him. The arrangements were made in such secret that he could only say farewell to his congregation by letter, in which he exhorted them not to give way to bitterness under persecution.

After traveling in Europe for a year, Howe realized he still could not return to England, so he settled in Utrecht, the Netherlands. He preached occasionally in the English church in

Utrecht and oversaw the theological studies of several English students at the University of Utrecht. Bishop Burnet, the historian, visited Howe in Utrecht. William of Orange, who later became king of England, also befriended Howe. The prince, who admired Cromwell, wanted to hear everything that Howe could tell him about the Protector.

In 1687, James II published the Declaration of Indulgence suspending penal laws against Roman Catholics and Protestant Dissenters. Howe's congregation sent him letters, pleading with him to return, but William warned Howe that this was another strategy for the Roman Catholics to gain influence. Howe returned home, only to discover that William was right. The king would have been greatly strengthened if Howe had been willing to declare the legality of the royal dispensing power, but Howe refused to do that. He and the majority of the Dissenters saw that toleration based upon the king's overruling of Parliament would have no lasting force. Soon, the king offended the majority of his subjects by attacking the liberty of the church and the prerogatives of Parliament. Leading men of the kingdom invited William to occupy the throne. On November 5, 1688, William landed at Torbay. Howe led the deputation of dissenting ministers who greeted William, and, in a moving address, assured him of their support.

Howe hoped that a ruling would be passed granting toleration to dissenters within the Church of England, but the House of Commons threw out the bill. Howe published his concerns in *The Case of the Protestant Dissenters Represented and Argued*, emphasizing agreement in doctrine between church and dissent, and how it was wrong to impose uniformity of worship upon those whose consciences led them in another direction.

Despite their efforts, the dissenters gained minimal toleration. The Act of Toleration exempted them from persecution for not attending their parish churches. They could build meetinghouses and use them for worship, provided they registered them with the authorities. Dissenters, however, were still barred from state or municipality offices, and universities were closed to them. Nevertheless they were grateful for the relief offered by the act. In response, Howe published *Humble Request to both Conformists and Dissenters touching their temper and behaviour towards each other upon the lately passed Indulgence*, showing that he was more concerned with the fellowship of Christians than with the advantage of any ecclesiastical party.

Howe was fifty-nine years old when the Act of Toleration was passed. In 1690, he and others drew up "Heads of Agreement between Presbyterians and Congregationalists," but it was in vain. Disputes between Calvinists and Arminians and arguments about the writings of Tobias Crisp complicated the situation. Theological pamphlet wars and debates entered the fray. Howe remained on the cutting edge of current discussions on predestination, the Trinity, and conformity, often writing books or lecturing at the weekly Broad Street Merchants' Lecture on such subjects. His last book, *Of Patience in Expectation of Future Blessedness*, was published in 1705, the year of his death.

Meantime, Howe continued preaching twice each Sabbath at Silver Street. The closer he came to death, the more his fellowship with God increased. At the last Communion that he administered, he so dwelt on heaven that some people were afraid that he would die during the service.

Like many Puritans, Howe was blessed with the presence of God in the midst of excruciating pain. "I expect my salvation," Howe said, "not as a profitable servant, but as a pardoned sinner." Once he told his wife that though he thought he loved her as well "as it was fit for one creature to love another," yet if he had to choose whether to die that moment or live for another seven years, he would choose to die. After a temporary respite, he pointed to his body and said, "I am for feeling that I am alive, and yet I am most willing to die and to lay aside this clog."

Before he died, Howe made his son George promise that he would burn all his private papers, except for his sermons and manuscripts, "stitched up in a number of small volumes." Consequently, few of Howe's numerous letters survived. Those that did survive are printed in Henry Rogers's *Life and Character of John Howe* (London: Religious Tract Society, 1863), the definitive biography on Howe, which Solid Ground Christian Books plans to reprint in the Fall of 2005.

Howe's dying words were those of one who already belonged to another world. As one biographer says, "He dwelt with great frequency, and almost superhuman eloquence, upon his favorite theme, the happiness of heaven, and spake as if he were already in the veil." Howe had several remarkable visits with Richard Cromwell, in which the tears of both men flowed freely as they conversed about the glory of the life to come. On April 2, 1705, God granted Howe his wish. He died without a struggle.

The Redeemer's Tears Wept over Lost Souls, this moving book, first printed in 1683, contains Howe's essay on Luke 19:41–42, telling how Jesus wept over Jerusalem because the city didn't recognize what belonged to peace in its day. It begins with a long exposition on the great gospel truths that "belong to men's peace." It then focuses on the short "day" we have in this life, which will decide our eternal destiny. It admonishes readers to flee to the willing, yearning Savior.

This is Howe's most searching and compelling book for wooing a sinner to Christ. He stresses the responsibility of man within the framework of divine sovereignty. It makes for a compelling read. We are grateful to Solid Ground Christian Books for bringing it back into print this century.

Joel R. Beeke
Puritan Reformed Theological Seminary
Grand Rapids, Michigan

Table of Contents

PREFACE

WHEN spiritual judgments do more eminently befall a people great outward calamities do often ensue. We know it was so in the instance which the text here insisted on refers to. But it is not always so ; the connexion between these two sorts of judgments is not absolutely certain and necessary, yea, and is more frequent with the contraries of each. For this reason therefore, and because judgments of the former kind are so inexpressibly greater and more tremendous, this discourse insists only upon them, about which serious monitions both have a clearer ground, and are of greater importance ; and wholly waives the latter.

Too many are apt, first to fancy similitudes between the state of things with one people and another, and then to draw inferences ; being perhaps imposed on by a strong imagination in both ; which yet must pass with them for a spirit of prophecy, and perhaps they take it not well, if it do not so with others too. It were indeed the work of another prophet certainly to accommodate and make application of what was spoken by a former to a distinct time and people. 'Tis enough for us to learn from such sayings as this of our Saviour, those rules of life and practice, such instruction and cautions as are common to all times, without arrogating to ourselves his prerogative, of foretelling events that shall happen in this or that. The affectation of venturing upon futurity, and foreboding direful things to kingdoms and nations, may, besides its being without sufficient ground, proceed from some one or other very bad principle. Dislike of the present methods of Providence, weariness and impatiency of our present condition, too great proneness to wish what we take upon us to predict, the prediction importing more heat of anger than certainty of foresight, a wrathful spirit, that would presently fetch down fire from heaven upon such as favour not our inclinations and desires, so that (as the poet speaks) whole cities should be overturned at our request, if the heavenly powers would be so easy, as to comply with such furious imprecations : a temper that ill agrees with humanity itself, not to care at what rate of common calamity and misery a purchase be made of our own immunity from sufferings. Nay, to be willing to run the most desperate hazard in the case, and even covet a general ruin to others, upon a mere apprehended possibility that our case may be mended by it ; when it may be more probable to become much worse. But O how disagreeable is it to the Spirit of our merciful Lord and Saviour, whose name we bear, upon any terms to delight in human miseries ! The greatest honour men of that complexion are capable of doing the Christian name, were to disclaim it. Can such angry heats have place in Christian breasts, as shall render them the well-pleased spectators, yea authors, of one another's calamities and ruin ? Can the tears that issued from these compassionate, blessed eyes, upon the foresight of Jerusalem's woful catastrophe, do nothing towards the quenching of these flames ?

But I add, that the too intent fixing of our thoughts upon any supposable events in this world, argues, at least, a narrow, carnal mind, that draws and gathers all things into time, as despairing of eternity ; and reckons no better state of things considerable, that is not to be brought about under their own present view, in this world ; as if it were uncertain or insignificant, that there shall be unexceptionable, eternal order and rectitude in another.

'Tis again as groundless, and may argue as ill a mind, to prophesy smooth and pleasant things, in a time of abounding wickedness. The safer, middle course, is, without God's express warrant, not to prophesy at all, but as we have opportunity, to warn and instruct men, with all meekness and long-suffering; for which the Lord's ordinary messengers can never want his warrant. And, after our blessed Saviour's most imitable example, to scatter our tears over the impenitent, even upon the (too probable) apprehension of the temporal judgments which hang over their heads, but most of all upon the account of their liableness to the more dreadful ones of the other state; which in the following discourse, I hope, it is made competently evident, this lamentation of our Saviour hath ultimate reference unto. For the other, though we know them to be due, and most highly deserved; yet concerning the actual infliction of them, even upon obstinate and persevering sinners, we cannot pronounce. We have no settled constitution, or rule, by which we can conclude it, any more than that outward felicity, or prosperity, shall be the constant portion of good men in this world. The great God hath reserved to himself a latitude of acting more arbitrarily, both as to promises and threatenings of this nature. If the accomplishment of either could be certainly expected, it should be of the promises rather; because as to promised rewards God is pleased to make himself debtor, and a right accrues to them to whom the promise is made, if either the promise be absolute, or made with any certain condition, that is actually performed. But God is always the *creditor pœnæ, the right to punish* remains wholly in himself, the exacting whereof he may therefore suspend, without any appearance of wrong, as seemeth good unto him. If, therefore, he may withhold temporal blessings from good and pious men, to which they have a remote and fundamental right, as having reserved to himself the judgment of the fit time and season of bestowing them; much more doth it belong to his wisdom, to fix the bounds of his patience and long-suffering; and determine the season of animadverting upon more open and insolent offenders by temporal punishments, according as shall make most for the ends of his government, and finally prove more advantageous to the dignity and glory of it. The practice, therefore, of our Saviour, in speaking so positively concerning the approaching fall and ruin of Jerusalem, is no pattern unto us. He spake not only with the knowledge of a prophet, but with the authority of a judge : and his words may be considered both as a prediction and a sentence. We can pretend to speak in neither capacity touching things of this nature.

But for the everlasting punishments in another world, that belong to unreconciled sinners, who refuse to know the things of their peace, the gospel-constitution hath made the connexion firm and unalterable, between their continuing, unrepented wickedness, and those punishments. When, therefore, we behold the impudent, provoking sins of the age wherein we live, against the natural law of our Creator, persisted in with all the marks of infidelity and obduration against the truth and grace that so gloriously shine forth in the gospel of our Redeemer, we may (after him) speak positively, He that believeth not shall be damned—is condemned already ; shall not see life, but the wrath of God abideth on him. If ye believe not that I am *He*, ye shall die in your sins. Except ye repent, ye shall all likewise perish. And here, how doth it become us too, in conformity to his great example, to speak compassionately, and as those that, in some measure, know the terror of the Lord ! O how doleful is the case, when we consider the inconsistent notions of many, with, not this or that particular doctrine, or article of the Christian faith, but with the whole sum of Christianity, the atheism of some, the avowed mere theism of others ! The former sort far outdoing the Jewish infidelity. Which people, besides the rational means of demonstrating a Deity common to them with the rest of mankind, could, upon the account of many things peculiar to themselves, be in no suspense concerning this matter. How great was their reverence of the books of the Old Testament, especially those of Moses ! their knowledge most certain of plain, and most convincing matter of fact. How long the government of their nation had been an immediate theocracy ! what evident tokens of the divine presence had been among them from age to age ! in how wonderful a manner they were brought out of Egypt, through the

Red sea, and conducted all along through the wilderness! how glorious an appearance and manifestation of himself God afforded to them at the giving of the law, upon mount Sinai! and by how apparent exertions of the divine power the former inhabitants were expelled, and they settled in the promised land! Upon all this they could be in no more doubt concerning the existence of a Deity, than of the sun in the firmament. Whereas we are put to prove, in a Christian nation, that this world, and its continual successive inhabitants, have a wise intelligent Maker and Lord, and that all things came not into the state wherein they are, by (no man can imagine what) either fatal necessity or casualty.

But both sorts agree in (what I would principally remark) the disbelief of Christ being the Messiah. And so, with both, the whole business of Christianity must be a fable and a cheat. And thus it is determined, not by men that have made it their business to consider and examine the matter (for the plain evidence of things cannot but even obtrude a conviction upon any diligent inquirer), but by such as have only resolved to consider; who have before-hand settled their purpose, never to be awed by the apprehension of an invisible Ruler, into any course of life that shall bear hard upon sensual inclination, have already chosen their master, enslaved themselves to brutal appetite, and are so habituated to that mean servility, made it so connatural, so deeply inward to themselves, so much their very life, as that through the pre-apprehended pain and uneasiness of a violent rupture, in tearing themselves from themselves, it is become their interest not to admit any serious thought. Any such thought they are concerned (they reckon) to fence against, as against the point of a sword; it strikes at their only life, the brute must die, that (by a happy $\pi\alpha\lambda\iota\gamma$-$\gamma\epsilon\nu\eta\sigma\iota\alpha$) they may be again born men. That is the design of Christianity, to restore men to themselves again; and because it hath this tendency, it is therefore not to be endured. And all the little residue of human wit which is yet left them (which because the sensual nature is predominant, is pressed into a subserviency to the interest and defence of a brutal life), only serves them to turn every thing of serious religion into ridicule, and being themselves resolved never to be reasoned into any seriousness, they have the confidence to make the trial, whether all other men can be jested out of it.

If this were not the case, if such persons could allow themselves to think and debate the matter, how certain would the victory, how glorious would the triumph be, of the Christian religion over all the little cavils they are wont to allege against it ! Let their own consciences testify in the case, whether ever they have applied themselves to any solemn disquisition concerning this important affair, but only contented themselves with being able, amidst transient discourse, to cast out, now and then, some oblique glance, against somewhat or other that was appendant, or more remotely belonging, to the Christian profession (in so much haste as not to stay for an answer), and because they may have surprised, sometimes, one or other, not so ready at a quick repartee, or who reckoned the matter to require solemn and somewhat larger discourse (which they have not had the patience to hear), whether they have not gone away puffed and swollen with the conceit, that they have whiffled Christianity away, quite off the stage, with their profane breath ; as if its firm and solid strength, wherein it stands stable, as a rock of adamant, depended upon this or that sudden, occasional, momentary effort on the behalf of it. But if such have a mind to try whether any thing can be strongly said in defence of that sacred profession, let them considerately peruse what hath been written by divers to that purpose. And not to engage them in any very tedious longsome task, if they like not to travel through the somewhat abstruser work of the most learned Hugo Grotius, *De Veritate Christianæ Religionis,* or the more voluminous Huetius, his *Demonstratio Evangelica,* or divers others that might be named, let them but patiently and leisurely read over that later very plain and clear, but nervous and solid, discourse of Dr Parker, upon this subject, and judge then, whether the Christian religion want evidence, or whether nothing can be alleged, why we of this age, so long after Christ's appearance upon the stage of the world, are to reckon ourselves obliged to profess Christianity, and observe the rules of that holy profession.

And really if, upon utmost search, it shall be found to have firm truth at the bottom, it makes itself so necessary (which must be acknowledged part of that truth), that any one that hath wit enough to be author of a jest, might understand it to be a thing not to be jested with. It trifles with no man. And, where it is once sufficiently propounded, leaves it no longer indifferent whether we will be of it or no. Supposing it true, it is strange if we can pretend it not to be sufficiently propounded to us; or that we are destitute of sufficient means to come by the knowledge of that truth! Was this religion instituted only for one nation or age? Did the Son of God descend from heaven, put on flesh, and die? had we an incarnate Deity conversant among men on earth, and made a sacrifice for the sins of men? and hath he left the world at liberty, whether, upon any notice hereof, they should inquire and concern themselves about him or no? Being incarnate he could not, as such, be every where; nor was it fit he should be long here, or needful (and, therefore, not fit) he should die often. It was condescension enough that he vouchsafed once to appear, in so mean and self-abasing a form, and offered himself to put away sin by the sacrifice of himself. And whereas he hath himself founded a dominion over us in his own blood, did die, and revive, and rise again, that he might be Lord of the living and of the dead; and the eternal Father hath hereupon highly exalted him, given him a name above every name, that at his name every knee should bow, and that all should confess that he is Lord, to the praise and glory of God; and hath required that all should honour the Son as himself is to be honoured; hath given him power over all flesh, and made him head of all things to the church: was it ever intended men should, generally, remain exempt from obligation to observe, believe, and obey him?

was it his own intention to waive, or not insist upon, his own most sacred, and so dearly acquired rights? to quit his claim to the greatest part of mankind? Why did he then issue out his commission as soon as he was risen from the dead, to teach all nations, to proselyte the world to himself, to baptize them into his name, with that of the Father and the Holy Ghost? (O the great and venerable names that are named upon professing Christians!) Could it be his intention, to leave it lawful to men to choose this, or any, or no religion, as their humours, or fancies, or lusts should prompt them; to disregard and deride his holy doctrines, violate and trample upon his just and equal laws, reject and contemn his offered favours and mercy, despise and profane his sacred institutions? When he actually makes his demand, and lays his claim, what amazing guilt, how swift destruction, must they incur, that dare adventure to deny the Lord that bought them! And they that shall do it, among a Christianized people, upon the pretended insufficiency of the revelation they have of him, do but heighten the affront and increase the provocation. 'Tis to charge the whole Christian institution with foolery, as pretending to oblige men, when they cannot know to what, how, or upon what ground they should be obliged; to pronounce the means and methods inept, and vain, which he hath thought sufficient (and only fit) for the propagating and continuing Christianity in the world; to render the rational reception of it from age to age impossible, in his appointed way; or unless men should be taught by angels, or voices from heaven, or that miracles should be so very frequent and common, as thereby also to become useless to their end; and so would be to make the whole frame of Christian religion an idle impertinency; and, in reference to its avowed design, a self-repugnant thing; and consequently were to impute folly to him who is the Wisdom of God.

And how are other things known, of common concernment, and whereof an immediate knowledge is as little possible? Can a man satisfy himself that he hath a title to an estate, conveyed down to him by very ancient writings,

the witnesses whereof are long since dead and gone ? or that
he is obliged by laws made many an age ago ? Or could
any records be preserved with more care and concern, than
those wherein our religion lies ? or be more secure from
designed or material deprivation ? But this is no place to
reason these things. Enough is said by others, referred to
before. I only further say, if any that have the use of
their understandings, living in a Christian nation, think to
justify their infidelity and disobedience to the Son of God,
by pretending they had no sufficient means to know him
to be so, the excuse will avail them alike, as that did him,
who insolently said, Who is the Lord, that I should obey
his voice ? I know not the Lord, neither will I, &c. For
have not we as good means to know who Christ is, as the
Egyptians at that time had, to know who was the God of
Israel, though afterwards he was more known by the judgments which he executed ? Although the knowledge of
the only true God be natural, and the obligation thereto
common to them ; yet the indisposition to use their understanding this way, is so great and general, and the express
revelation that Jesus Christ was the Son of God, requires so
much less labour to understand it, than there is in arguing
out the existence and attributes of God, by an inhabile,
sluggish mind, that the difference cannot be great, if any,
on that side. This latter only needs the inquiry, whence
the revelation comes ; which as it is not difficult in itself,
so this occasion, viz. of its being proposed, doth invite and
urge to it ; whereas the generality of the pagan world have
little of external inducement, leading them into inquiries
concerning the true God. Therefore, all circumstances
considered, I see not how they that live under the gospel
can be thought to have less advantage and obligation to
own Jesus of Nazareth to be the Son of God, than the rest
of the world, to own the only living and true God ; or that
the former should be less liable to the revelation of the
wrath of God from heaven for holding supernatural truth
in unrighteousness, than the other, for doing so injurious
violence to that which is merely natural. Unto what

severities, then, of the divine wrath and justice, even of the highest kind, do multitudes lie open in our days !

For besides those (much fewer) mental, or notional, infidels, that believe not the principles of the Christian religion, against the clearest evidence, how vastly greater is the number of them that are so in heart and practice, against their professed belief ! that live in utter estrangement from God, as without him in the world, or in open enmity against him, and contrariety to the known rules of the religion they profess !   How many that understand nothing of its principal and plainest doctrines ! as if nothing were requisite to distinguish the Christian from the pagan world, more than an empty name ; or as if the Redeemer of sinners had died upon the cross, that men might more securely remain alienated from the life of God, not to reconcile and reduce them to him ! or that they might with safety indulge appetite, mind earthly things, make the world their god, gratify the flesh, and make provision to fulfil the lusts of it, defy heaven, affront their Maker, live in malice, envy, hatred to one another ! not to bless them, by turning them from these impieties and iniquities !   As if it were so obscurely hinted, as that it could not be taken notice of, that the grace of God, which bringeth salvation to all men, hath appeared, teaching them to deny ungodliness and worldly lusts, and to live soberly, righteously, and godly in this present world, so looking for the blessed hope. And that Christ gave himself for us, to redeem us from all iniquity, and to purify us to himself a peculiar people, zealous of good works !   How many, again, are Christians, they know not why ! upon the same terms that others are Mahometans, because it is the religion of their country, by fate or by accident, not by their own choice and judgment !   The same inconsideration makes them be Christians, that makes others be none.

And now, shall our Redeemer be left to weep alone over these perishing souls ? have we no tears to spend upon this doleful subject ?   Oh that our heads were waters, and our eyes fountains !   Is it nothing to us, that multitudes are sinking, going down into perdition, under the name of

Christian, under the seal of baptism, from under the means of life and salvation ! perishing ! and we can do nothing to prevent it ? We know they must perish that do not repent and turn to God, and love him above all, even with all their hearts and souls, and mind and might ; that do not believe in his Son and pay him homage, as their rightful Lord, sincerely subjecting themselves to his laws and government. But this they will not understand, or not consider. Our endeavours to bring them to it are ineffectual ; 'tis but faint breath we utter. Our words drop and die between us and them ! We speak to them in the name of the eternal God that made them, of the great Jesus who bought them with his blood, and they regard it not. The Spirit of the Lord is in a great degree departed from among us, and we take it not to heart ! We are sensible of lesser grievances, are grieved that men will not be more entirely proselyted to our several parties and persuasions, rather than that they are so disinclined to become proselytes to real *Christianity ;* and seem more deeply concerned to have Christian religion so or so modified, than whether there shall be any such thing ! or whether men be saved by it or lost !

This sad case, that so many were likely to be lost under the first sound of the gospel ; and the most exemplary temper of our blessed Lord in reference to it, are represented in the following treatise ; with design to excite their care for their own souls, who need to be warned, and the compassions of others for them who are so little apt to take warning. The good Lord grant that it may be, some way or other, useful for good !

JOHN HOWE

THE REDEEMER'S TEARS

WEPT OVER LOST SOULS

*"And when he was come near, he beheld the city, and wept over it, saying,
If thou hadst known, even thou, at least in this thy day, the things which
belong unto thy peace ! but now they are hid from thine eyes."*—Luke,
xix. 41, 42.

WE have here a compassionate lamentation in the midst
of a solemn triumph. Our Lord's approach unto Jerusalem at this time, and his entrance into it (as the foregoing
history shews), carried with them some face of regal and
triumphal pomp, but with such allays, as discovered a
mind most remote from ostentation ; and led by judgment
(not vain glory), to transmit through a dark umbrage some
glimmerings only of that excellent majesty which both his
sonship and his mediatorship entitled him unto ; a very
modest and mean specimen of his true indubious royalty
and kingly state ; such as might rather intimate than
plainly declare it, and rather afford an after-instruction to
teachable minds, than beget a present conviction and dread
in the stupidly obstinate and unteachable. And this effect
we find it had, as is observed by another evangelical historian ; who relating the same matter, how in his passage to
Jerusalem the people met him with branches of palm-
trees and joyful hosannas, he riding upon an ass's colt
(as princes or judges, to signify meekness as much as state,
were wont to do, Judges v. 10), tells us, these things his
disciples understood not at the first, but when Jesus was
glorified, then remembered they that these things were
written of him, and that they had done these things unto
him, John, xii. 16. For great regard was had in this, as

in all the acts of his life and ministry, to that last and conclusive part, his dying a sacrifice upon the c·oss for the sins of men ; to observe all along that mediocrity, and steer that middle course between obscurity and a terrifying, overpowering glory, that this solemn oblation of himself might neither be prevented, nor be disregarded. Agreeably to this design, and the rest of his course, he doth, in this solemnity, rather discover his royal state and dignity by a dark emblem, than by an express representation ; and shews in it more of meekness and humility, than of awful majesty and magnificence, as was formerly predicted, Zech. ix. 9. Rejoice greatly, O daughter of Zion ; shout, O daughter of Jerusalem : behold, thy King cometh unto thee : he is just, and having salvation ; lowly, and riding upon an ass, and upon a colt the foal of an ass.

And how little he was taken in this piece of state, is sufficiently to be seen in this paragraph of the chapter. His mind is much more taken up in the foresight of Jerusalem's sad case ; and therefore being come within view of it (which he might very commodiously have in the descent of the higher opposite hill, mount Olivet), he beheld the city, 'tis said, and wept over it. Two things concur to make up the cause of this sorrow :—1. The greatness of the calamity ; Jerusalem, once so dear to God, was to suffer, not a scar, but a ruin ;—" The days shall come upon thee, that thine enemies shall cast a trench about thee, and compass thee in on every side, and shall lay thee even with the ground, and thy children within thee ; and they shall not leave in thee one stone upon another :" and—2. The lost opportunity of preventing it ;—" If thou hadst known, even thou, at least in this thy day, the things which belong unto thy peace ! but now they are hid from thine eyes," ver. 42. And again, " Thou knewest not the time of thy visitation."

First, The calamity was greater in his eyes, than it can be in ours. His large and comprehensive mind could take the compass of this sad case. Our thoughts cannot reach far, yet we can apprehend what may make this case very deplorable ; we can consider Jerusalem as the city of the great King, where was the palace and throne of the Majesty of heaven, vouchsafing to "dwell with men on earth." Here the divine light and glory had long shone ; here was the sacred Shechinah, the dwelling-place of the Most High, the symbols of his presence, the seat of worship, the mercy-seat, the place of receiving addresses, and of dispensing favours ; "The house of prayer for all nations." To his own people this was the city of their solemnities, whither the tribes were wont to go up, the tribes of the Lord, unto the testimony of Israel, to give thanks unto the name of the Lord : for there were set thrones of judgment, the thrones of the house of David, Psal. cxxii. 4, 5. He that was so great a lover of the souls of men, how grateful and dear to his heart had the place been where through the succession of many by-past ages the great God did use (though more obscurely) to unfold his kind intentions towards sinners, to hold solemn treaties with them, to make himself known, to draw and allure souls into his own holy worship and acquaintance ! And that now the dismal prospect presents itself of desolation and ruin, ready to overwhelm all this glory ! and lay waste the dwellings of divine love ! his sorrow must be conceived proportionable to the greatness of this desolating change.

Secondly, And the opportunity of prevention was quite lost ! There was an opportunity : "He was sent to the lost sheep of the house of Israel : he came to them as his own." Had they received him, O how joyful a place had Jerusalem been ! How glorious had the triumphs of God been there, had they repented, believed, obeyed These were the "things that belonged to their peace ;" this was their opportunity, their "day of visitation ;" these were the things that might have been done within that day : but it was now too late, their day was over, and the things of their peace hid from their eyes ; and how fervent were his desires, they had done otherwise ! taken the wise and safe course. If thou hadst known ! the words admit the optative form, εἰ being put, as 'tis observed to be sometimes by other authors, for εἴθε, *utinam ;* O that thou hadst known, I wish thou hadst ; his sorrow must be proportionable to his love. Or otherwise we may conceive the sentence incomplete, part cut off by a more emphatical *aposiopesis*, tears interrupting speech, and imposing a more speaking silence, which imports an affection beyond all words. They that were anciently so over-officious as to raze those words " and wept over it" out of the canon, as thinking it unworthy so divine a person to shed tears, did greatly err, not knowing the Scriptures (which elsewhere speak of our Lord's weeping), nor the power of divine love, (now become incarnate), nor indeed the true perfections and properties of human nature : otherwise they had never taken upon them to reform the gospel, and reduce not only Christianity, but Christ himself, to the measures and square of their stoical philosophy : but these have also met with a like ancient confutation.

One thing (before we proceed) needs some disquisition, viz.—Whether this lamentation of our blessed Lord do refer only or ultimately to the temporal calamity he foresaw coming upon Jerusalem :—or whether it had not a further and more principal reference to their spiritual and eternal miseries that were certain to be concomitant, and consequent thereunto ? Where let it be considered,

1. That very dreadful spiritual plagues and judgments did accompany their destruction very generally ; which every one knows who is acquainted with their after-story, *i. e.* that takes notice what spirit reigned among them, and what their behaviour was towards our Lord himself, and afterwards towards his apostles and disciples all along to their fearful catastrophe ; (as it may be collected from the sacred records, and other history) ; what blindness of mind, what hardness of heart, what mighty prejudice, what inflexible obstinacy, against the clearest light, the largest mercy, the most perspicuous and most gracious doctrine, and the most glorious works, wrought to confirm it, against the brightest beams and evidences of the divine truth, love, and power ! what persevering impenitency and infi-

delity against God and Christ, proceeding from the bitterest enmity ! (Ye have both seen and hated me and my Father, John, xv. 24). What mad rage and fury against one another, even when death and destruction were at the very door ! Here were all the tokens imaginable of the most tremendous infatuation, and of their being forsaken of God. Here was a concurrence of all kinds of spiritual judgments in the highest degree.

2. That the concomitancy of such spiritual evils with their temporal destruction, our Lord foreknew as well as their temporal destruction itself. It lay equally in view before him ; and was as much under his eye. He that knew what was in man, could as well tell what would be in him. And by the same light by which he could immediately look into hearts, he could as well see into futurities, and as well the one futurity as the other. The knowledge of the one he did not owe to his human understanding : from his divine understanding, whereby he knew all things, the other could not be hid.

3. The connexion between the impenitency and infidelity that prove to be final, and eternal misery, is known to us all. Of his knowlege of it therefore (whose law hath made the connexion, besides what there is in the nature of the things themselves) there can be no doubt.

4. That the miseries of the soul, especially such as prove incurable and eternal, are in themselves far the greatest, we all acknowledge : nor can we make a difficulty to believe, that our Lord apprehended and considered things according as they were in themselves, so as to allow every thing its own proper weight and import in his estimating of them. These things seem all very evident to any eye. Now though it be confessed not impossible, that of things so distinct from one another as outward and temporal evils, and those that are spiritual and eternal, even befalling the same persons, one may for the present consider the one without attending to the other, or making distinct reflection thereon at the same time ; yet how unlikely is it, these things bordering so closely upon one another as they did in the pre-

sent case, that so comprehensive a mind as our Saviour's was, sufficiently able to enclose them both, and so spiritual a mind, apt no doubt to consider most what was in itself most considerable, should in a solemn lamentation of so sad a case, wholly overlook the saddest part, and stay his thoughts only upon the surface and outside of it ! That he mentions only the approaching outward calamity (ver. 43, 44), was that he spake in the hearing of the multitude, and upon the way, but in passing, when there was not opportunity for large discourse ; and therefore he spake what might soonest strike their minds, was most liable to common apprehension, and might most deeply affect ordinary, and not yet enough prepared, hearers.

And he spake what he had, no doubt, a deep sense of himself. Whatever of tender compassions might be expected from the most perfect humanity and benignity, could not be wanting in him, upon the foresight of such a calamity as was coming upon that place and people. But yet, what was the sacking of a city, the destroying of pompous buildings that were all of a perishable material, the mangling of human flesh, over which the worm was otherwise shortly to have had dominion ; to the alienation of men's minds from God, their disaffection to the only means of their recovery, and reconciliation to him, and their subjection to his wrath and curse for ever ! When also it is plain he considered that perverse temper of mind and spirit in them, as the cause of their ruin ! which his own words imply ; that " the things which belonged to their peace were hid from their eyes ;" and that the things he foretold, should befall them, because " they knew not the time of their visitation." For what could the things be that belonged to their peace, but turning to God, believing in himself, as the Messiah, bringing forth the fruits meet for repentance ? Whence also there must be another latent and concealed meaning of their peace itself, than only their continued amity with the Roman state ; their peace with heaven ; their being set right, and standing in favour and acceptance, with God. For was it ever the first intention of the things enjoined in gospel, but to entitle men to earthly secular benefits ?

Nor can we doubt but the same things lay deep in the mind of our blessed Lord, when he uttered these words, as when he spake those so very like them, Matt. xxiii. 37, 38. O Jerusalem, Jerusalem, thou that killest the prophets, and stonest them which are sent unto thee, how often would I have gathered thy children together even as a hen gathereth her chickens under her wings, and ye would not! Behold, your house is left unto you desolate. These other were not spoken indeed at the same time, but very soon after : *those* we are considering, in his way to the city, *these* when he was come into it, most probably, by the series of the evangelical history, the second day, after his having lodged the first night at Bethany. But it is plain they have the same sense, and that the same things lay with great weight upon his spirit ; so that the one passage may contribute much to the enlightening and expounding of the other.

Now what can be meant by that, " I would have gathered you as the hen her chickens under her wings ?" Could it intend a political meaning ; that he would have been a temporal prince and saviour to them ? which he so earnestly declined and disclaimed ; professing to the last, his kingdom was not of this world. It could mean no other thing, but that he would have reduced them back to God, have gathered and united them under his own gracious and safe conduct in order thereto, have secured them from the divine wrath and justice, and have conferred on them spiritual and eternal blessings. In a like sense their *peace* here was no doubt more principally to be understood; and their loss and forfeiture of it, by their not understanding the things belonging thereto, considered and lamented.

Therefore the principal intendment of this lamentation, though directly applied to a community, and the formed body of a people, is equally applicable unto particular persons living under the gospel, or to whom the ordinary means of conversion and salvation are vouchsafed, but are neglected by them and forfeited. We may therefore thus sum up the meaning and sense of these words :—That it is a thing in itself very lamentable, and much lamented by our Lord Jesus, when such as living under the gospel, have had a day of grace, and an opportunity of knowing the things belonging to their peace, have so outworn that day, and lost their opportunity, that the things of their peace are quite hid from their eyes :—where we have these distinct heads of discourse to be severally considered and insisted on.

I. What are the things necessary to be known by such as live under the gospel, as immediately belonging to their peace.

II. That they have a day or season wherein to know not these things only, but the whole compass of their case, and what the knowledge of those things more immediately belonging to their peace supposes, and depends upon.

III. That this day hath its bounds and limits, so that when it is over and lost ; those things are for ever hid from their eyes.

IV. That this is a case to be considered with deep resentment and lamentation, and was so by our Lord Jesus.

I. What are the things necessary to be known by such as live under the gospel, as immediately belonging to their peace ? Where we are more particularly to inquire,—1. What those things themselves are—2. What sort of knowledge of them it is that here is meant, and made necessary.

1. What the things are which belong to the peace of a people living under the gospel. The things belonging to a people's peace, are not throughout the same with all. Living, or not living, under the gospel makes a considerable difference in the matter. Before the incarnation and public appearance of our Lord, something was not necessary among the Jews, that afterwards became necessary. It was sufficient to them before, to believe in a Messiah to come, more indefinitely. Afterwards he plainly tells them, If ye believe not that I am he, ye shall die in your sins, John, viii. 24. Believing in Christ cannot be necessary to

pagans that never heard of him, *as a duty*, howsoever necessary it may be *as a means*. Their not believing in him
cannot be itself a sin, though by it they should want remedy for their other sins. But it more concerns us who
do live under the gospel, to apprehend aright what is necessary for ourselves. That is a short and full summary
which the Apostle gives, Acts, xx. 21. Repentance towards
God, and faith in our Lord Jesus Christ. The gospel finds
us in a state of apostacy from God, both as our sovereign
Ruler, and sovereign Good, not apt to obey and glorify him,
as the former, nor enjoy him, and be satisfied in him, as
the latter. Repentance towards God cures and removes
this disaffection of our minds and hearts towards him,
under both these notions. By it the whole soul turns to
him, with this sense and resolution : " I have been a rebellious disloyal wretch, against the high authority and
most rightful government of him who gave me breath, and
whose creature I am. I will live no longer thus. Lo now
I come back unto thee, O Lord, thou art my Lord and
God. Thee I now design to serve and obey, as the Lord
of my life ; thee I will fear, unto thee I subject myself, to
live no longer after my own will, but thine. I have been
hitherto a miserable forlorn distressed creature, destitute of
any thing that could satisfy me, or make me happy ; have
set my heart upon a vain and thorny world, that had
nothing in it answerable to my real necessities, that hath
flattered and mocked me often, never satisfied me, and been
wont to requite my pursuits of satisfaction from it with
vexation and trouble, and ' pierce me through with many
sorrows.' I have borne in the mean time a disaffected
heart towards thee, have therefore cast thee out of my
thoughts, so that amidst all my disappointments and sorrows, it never came into my mind to say, ' Where is God
my Maker ?' I could never savour any thing spiritual
or divine, and was ever more ready, in distress, to turn
myself any way than (that which I ought) towards thee.
I now see and bemoan my folly, and with a convinced,
self-judging heart, betake myself to thee ; the desires of my

soul are now unto thy name, and to the remembrance of thee. Whom have I in heaven but thee, or on earth that I can desire besides thee ?"

This is " repentance towards God," and is one thing belonging, and most simply necessary, to our peace. But though it be most necessary, it is not enough. It answers to something of our wretched case, but not to every thing. We were in our state of apostasy averse and disaffected to God. To this evil, repentance towards him is the opposite and only proper remedy. But besides our being without inclination towards him, we are also without interest in him. We not only had unjustly cast off him, but were also most justly cast off by him. Our injustice had set us against him, and his justice had set him against us ; we need, in order to our peace with him, to be relieved as well against his justice, as our own injustice. What if, now we would return to him, he will not receive us ? And he will not receive us for our own sakes. He must have a recompense for the wrong we had done him, by our rebellion against his government, and our contempt of his goodness. Our repentance is no expiation. Nor have we of our own, or were capable of obliging him to give us, the power and grace to repent. Our high violation of the sacred rights and honour of the Godhead, made it necessary, in order to our peace and reconciliation, there should be a sacrifice, and a mediator between him and us. He hath judged it not honourable to him, not becoming him to treat with us, or vouchsafe us favours upon other terms. And since he thought it necessary to insist upon having a sacrifice, he judged it necessary too, to have one proportionable to the wrong done ; lest he should make the Majesty of heaven cheap, or occasion men to think it a light matter to have fundamentally overturned the common order which was settled between himself and men. The whole earth could not have afforded such a sacrifice, it must be supplied from heaven. His co-eternal Son made man, and so uniting heaven and earth in his own person, undertakes to be that sacrifice, and, in the virtue of it, to be a standing continual

Mediator between God and us; through him, and for his sake, all acts and influences of grace are to proceed towards us. No sin is to be forgiven, no grace to be conferred, but upon his account. 'Tis reckoned most God-like, most suitable to the divine greatness, once offended, to do nothing that shall import favour towards sinners, but upon his constant interposition. Him hath he set over us, and directed that all our applications to himself, and all our expectations from him, should be through him. Him hath he exalted to be a Prince and a Saviour, to give us repentance and remission of sins, Acts, v. 31. Now to one so high in power over us, he expects we should pay a suitable homage. That homage the Holy Scripture calls by the name of Faith, believing on him. God hath set him forth to be a propitiation, through faith in his blood, to declare his righteousness for the remission of sins that are past, through the forbearance of God; to declare his righteousness, that he might be just, and the justifier of him which believeth in Jesus, Rom. iii. 25, 26. So that when by repentance we turn to God, as our end, we must also apply ourselves by faith, to our Lord Jesus Christ, as our way to that end. Which till we do, we are in rebellion still, and know not what belongs to our peace. He insists that his Son, into whose hands he hath committed our affairs, should be honoured by us, as he himself requires to be, John, v. 23.

Now these two things sum up our part of the covenant between God and us. By repentance we again take God for our God. Repenting we return to him as our God. By faith we take his Son for our Prince and Saviour. These things, by the tenor of the evangelical covenant, are required of us. Peace is settled between God and us (as it is usually with men towards one another after mutual hostilities) by striking a covenant. And in our case it is a covenant by sacrifice, as you have seen. Nor are harder terms than these imposed upon us. Dost thou now, sinner, apprehend thyself gone off from God? and find a war is commenced and on foot, between God and thee? He can easily conquer and crush thee to nothing, but he offers thee terms of peace, upon which he is willing to enter into covenant with thee. Dost thou like his terms? Art thou willing to return to him, and take him again for thy God? to resign and commit thyself with unfeigned trust and subjection into the hands of his Son thy Redeemer? These are " the things which belong to thy peace." See that thou now know them.

2. But what knowledge of them is it that is here meant? The thing speaks itself. It is not a mere contemplative knowledge. We must so know them as to do them; otherwise the increase of knowledge is the increase of sorrow. Thy guilt and misery will be the greater. To know any thing that concerns our practice, is to no purpose if we do not practise it. It was a Hebrew form of speech, and is a common form, by words of knowledge to imply practice. It being taken for granted that in matters so very reasonable and important, if what we are to do once be rightly known, it will be done. Thus elsewhere the same great requisites to eternal life and blessedness are expressed by our Lord. This is life eternal, to know thee the only true God, and Jesus Christ whom thou hast sent; it being supposed and taken for granted that a true, vivid knowledge of God and Christ will immediately form the soul to all suitable dispositions and deportments towards the one and the other; and consequently to all men also, as Christian precepts do direct to all the acts of sobriety, justice, and charity, unto which the law of Christ obliges. An habitual course of sin in any kind, is inconsistent with this knowledge of the things of our peace, and therefore with our peace itself. All sin is in a true sense reducible to ignorance; and customary sinning into total destitution of divine knowledge. According to the usual style of the sacred writings, 1 Cor. xv. 34. Awake to righteousness, and sin not; for some have not the knowledge of God. 3 John ii. He that sinneth i. e. that is a doer of sin, ὁ κακοποιῶν, *a worker of iniquity*, hath not seen God.

II. Such as live under the gospel have a day, or a present opportunity, for the obtaining the knowledge of these

things immediately belonging to their peace, and of whatsoever is besides necessary thereunto. I say nothing what
opportunities they have who never lived under the gospel,
who yet no doubt might generally know more than they
do ; and know better what they do know. It suffices us
who enjoy the gospel, to understand our own advantages
thereby. Nor, as to those who do enjoy it, is every one's
day of equal clearness. How few in comparison, have ever
seen such a day as Jerusalem at this time did ! made by
the immediate beams of the Sun of righteousness ! our Lord
himself vouchsafing to be their Instructor, so speaking as
never man did ; and with such authority as far outdid their
other teachers, and astonished the hearers. In what trans-
ports did he use to leave those that heard him, wheresoever
he came, wondering at the gracious words that came out
of his mouth ! And with what mighty and beneficial works
was he wont to recommend his doctrine, shining in the
glorious power, and savouring of the abundant mercy of
heaven, so as every apprehensive mind might see the Deity
was incarnate, God was come down to treat with men, and
allure them into the knowledge and love of himself. The
word was made flesh. What unprejudiced mind might
not perceive it to be so ? He was there manifested and
veiled at once ; both expressions are used concerning the
same matter. The Divine beams were somewhat obscured,
but did yet ray through that vail ; so that his glory was
beheld as the glory of the only begotten Son of the Father,
full of grace and truth, John i. 14. This Sun shone with
a mild and benign, but with a powerful vivifying light.
In him was life, and that life was the light of men. Such
a light created unto the Jews this their day. Happy Jews,
if they had understood their own happiness ! And the days
that followed, to them (for a while) and the gentile world,
were not inferior, in some respects brighter and more glorious (the more copious gift of the Holy Ghost being reserved unto the crowning and enthroning of the victorious
Redeemer), when the everlasting gospel flew like lightning
to the utmost ends of the earth ; and the word which began

to be spoken by the Lord himself, was confirmed by them that heard him, God also himself bearing them witness, with signs, and wonders, and gifts of the Holy Ghost, Heb. ii. 4. No such day hath been seen this many an age. Yet whithersoever the same gospel, for substance, comes, it also makes a day of the same kind, and affords always true, though diminished light; whereby, however the things of our peace might be understood and known. The written gospel varies not; and if it be but simply and plainly proposed (though to some it be proposed with more advantage, to some with less, yet), still we have the same things immediately relating to our peace extant before our eyes; and divers things besides, which it concerns us to be acquainted with, that we may the more distinctly and to better purpose understand these things. For instance,

1. We have the true and distinct state of the quarrel between God and us. Pagans have understood somewhat of the apostasy of man from God; that he is not in the same state wherein he was at first. But while they have understood that something was amiss, they could scarce tell what. The gospel reveals the universal pravity of the degenerate nature even of all men, and of every faculty in man; That there is none that doeth good, no not one (Rom. iii.); and that every one is altogether become filthy and impure, and that there is an entire old man to be put off, wholly corrupt by deceivable lusts (Eph. iv.); that the ἀκρόπολις, the noblest powers, are vitiated, the mind and conscience defiled; that the spirit of the mind needs renewing, is sunk into carnality; and that the carnal mind is enmity against God (Rom. viii.), and is not subject to his law, nor can be, nor capable of savouring the things of God; that the sinner is in the flesh, under the dominion of power, and in the possession of the fleshly, sensual nature, and can therefore neither obey God nor enjoy him; that it is become impossible to him either to please God, or be pleased with him. That the sinner's quarrel therefore with God is about the most appropriate rights of the Godhead; the controversy is who shall be God, which is

the supreme authority and which is the supreme good.
The former peculiarity of the Godhead, the lapsed creature
is become so insolent, as to usurp and arrogate to himself.
When he is become so much less than a man (a very beast)
he will be a god. His sensual will shall be his only law.
He lives and walks after the flesh, serves divers lusts and
pleasures, and says, " Who is the Lord over me ?" But
being conscious that he is not self-sufficient, that he must
be beholden to somewhat foreign to himself for his satisfaction, and finding nothing else suitable to his sensual
inclination; that other divine peculiarity, to be the supreme
good, he places upon the sensible world ; and for this purpose *that* shall be his god ; so that between himself and
the world he attempts to share the undivided Godhead.
This is a controversy of a high nature, and about other
matters than even the Jewish Rabbins thought of, who
when Jerusalem was destroyed, supposed God was angry
with them for their neglect of the recitation of their phy-
lacteries morning and evening ; or that they were not respectful enough of one another ; or that distance enough
was not observed between superiors and inferiors, &c. The
gospel impleads men as rebels against their rightful Lord ;
but of this treason against the Majesty of heaven men little
suspect themselves till they are told. The gospel tells them
so plainly, represents the matter in so clear a light, that
they need only to contemplate themselves in that light, and
they may see that so it is. Men may indeed, by resolved,
stiff winking, create to themselves a darkness amidst the
clearest light. But open thine eyes man, thou that livest
under the gospel, set thyself to view thine own soul, thou wilt
find it is day with thee ; thou hast a day, by being under
the gospel, and light enough to see that this is the posture
of thy soul, and the state of thy case God-ward. And it is
a great matter towards the understanding the things of thy
peace, to know aright what is the true state of the quarrel
between God and thee.

2. The gospel affords light to know what the issue of
this quarrel is sure to be, if it go on, and there be no recon-

ciliation. It gives us other and plainer accounts of the punishment of the other world ; more fully represents the extremity and perpetuity of the future miseries, and state of perdition appointed for the ungodly world ; speaks out concerning the " Tophet prepared of old" (Isa. xxx.), " the lake of fire and brimstone" (Rev. xxi.) ; shews the miseries of that state to be the immediate effects of divine displeasure ; that " the breath of the Almighty as a river of brimstone" always foments those flames ; that " indignation and wrath cause the tribulation and anguish" (Rom. ii.) which must be the portion of evil-doers ; and how " fearful a thing it is to fall into the hands of the living God !" (Heb. x.) It gives us to understand what accession men's own unaltered vicious habits will have to their miseries ; their own outrageous lusts and passions, which here they made it their business to satisfy, becoming their insatiable tormentors ; that they are to receive " the *things done* in the body, according to what they have done" (2 Cor. v.) ; and that " what they have sowed, *the same* also they are to reap" (Gal. vi.) ; and what their own guilty reflections will contribute, the bitings and gnawings of the worm that dies not, the venomous corrosions of the viper bred in their own bosoms, and now become a full-grown serpent ; what the society and insultation of devils, with whom they are to partake in woes and torments, and by whom they have been seduced and trained into that cursed partnership and communion ; and that this fire wherein they are to be tormented together, is to be everlasting, " a fire never to be quenched." If men be left to their own conjectures only, touching the danger they incur by continuing and keeping up a war with heaven, and are to make their own hell, and that it be the creature only of their own imagination ; 'tis like they will make it as easy and favourable as they can ; and so are little likely to be urged earnestly to sue for peace by the imagination of a tolerable hell. But if they understand it to be altogether intolerable, this may make them bestir themselves, and think the favour of God worth the seeking. The gospel imports favour and kindness to you, when it imports most of terror, in telling you so plainly the worst of your case if you go on in a sinful course. It makes you a day, by which you may make a truer judgment of the blackness, darkness, and horror of that everlasting night that is coming on upon you ; and lets you know that black and endless night is introduced by a terrible preceding day, that day of the Lord the business whereof is judgment. They that live under the gospel cannot pretend they are in darkness so as that day should overtake them as a thief; and that, by surprise, they should be doomed and abandoned to the regions of darkness. The gospel forewarns you plainly of all this ; which it does not merely to fright and torment you before the time, but that you may steer your course another way, and escape the place and state of torment. It only says this that it may render the more acceptable to you what it hath to say besides ; and only threatens you with these things if there be no reconciliation between God and you. But then at the same time,

3. It also represents God to you as reconcilable through a Mediator. In that gospel " peace is preached to you, by Jesus Christ." That gospel lets you see God in Christ reconciling the world unto himself, that sin may not be imputed to them. That gospel proclaims glory to God in the highest, peace on earth, good will towards men. So did the voices of angels sum up the glad tidings of the gospel, when that Prince of peace was born into the world. It tells you " God desires not the death of sinners, but that they may turn and live ;" that he would " have all men be saved, and come to the knowledge of the truth ;" that he is " long-suffering towards them, not willing that any should perish, but that all should come to repentance," that he " so loved the world that he gave his only-begotten Son, that whosoever believes on him should not perish, but have everlasting life." The rest of the world can't but collect, from darker intimations, God's favourable propensions towards them. He spares them, is patient towards them, that herein " his goodness might lead them to

repentance." He sustains them, lets them dwell in a world which they might understand was of his making, and whereof he is absolute Lord. " They live, move, and have their being in him, that. they might seek after him, and by feeling find him out." He doth them " good, gives them rain from heaven and fruitful seasons, filling their hearts with food and gladness." He lets " his sun shine on them," whose far extended beams shew forth his kindness and benignity to men, even " to the utmost ends of the earth. For there is no speech or language whither his line and circle reaches not." But those are but dull and glimmering beams in comparison of those that shine from the Sun of righteousness through the gospel-revelation, and in respect of that divine glory which appears in the face of Jesus Christ. How clearly doth the light of this gospel-day reveal God's design of reducing sinners, and reconciling them to himself by a Redeemer ! How canst thou but say, sinner, thou hast a day of it ? and clear day-light shewing thee what the good and acceptable will of God towards thee is ? Thou art not left to guess only thou mayst be reconciled and find mercy, and to grope and feel thy way in the dark, unless it be a darkness of thy own making. And whereas a sinner, a disloyal rebellious creature, that hath affronted the Majesty of heaven, and engaged against himself the wrath and justice of his Maker, and is unable to make him any recompense, can have no reason to hope God will shew him mercy, and be reconciled to him for his own sake, or for any thing he can do to oblige or induce him to it ; the same gospel shews you plainly, it is for the Redeemer's sake, and what he hath done and suffered to procure it. But inasmuch also as the sinner may easily apprehend, that it can never answer the necessities of his state and case, that God only be not his enemy, that he forbear hostilities towards him, pursue him not with vengeance to his destruction. For he finds himself an indigent creature, and he needs somewhat beyond what he hath ever yet met with to make him happy ; that it is uneasy and grievous to wander up and down with craving desires among varieties of objects that look speciously, but which, either he cannot so far compass as to make a trial what there is in them, or wherewith, upon trial, he finds himself mocked and disappointed, and that really they have nothing in them ; he finds himself a mortal creature, and considers that if he had all that he can covet in this world, the increase of his present enjoyments doth but increase unto him trouble and anguish of heart, while he thinks what great things he must shortly leave and lose for ever, to go he knows not whither, into darksome, gloomy regions, where he cannot so much as imagine any thing suitable to his inclinations and desires. For he knows all that is delectable to his present sense he must here leave behind him ; and he cannot divest himself of all apprehensions of a future state, wherein if God should make him suffer nothing, yet, if he have nothing to enjoy, he must be *always* miserable.

4. The gospel, therefore, further represents to him the final, eternal blessedness, and glorious state, which they that are reconciled shall be brought into. They that live under the gospel are not mocked with shadows, and empty clouds, nor with fabulous elysiums. Nor are they put off with some unintelligible notion of only being happy in general. But are told expressly wherein their happiness is to consist. " Life and immortality are brought to light in the gospel." 'Tis given them to understand how great a good is laid up in store. The things which eye hath not seen, and ear not heard, and which otherwise could not have entered into the heart of man, the things of God's present and eternal kingdom, are set in view. It shews the future state of the reconciled shall consist not only in freedom from what is evil, but in the enjoyment of the best and most delectable good ; that God himself in all his glorious fulness will be their eternal and most satisfying portion ; that their blessedness is to lie in the perpetual fruitive vision of his blessed face, and in the fulness of joy, and the everlasting pleasures which the divine presence itself doth perpetually afford. And whereas their glorious

Redeemer is so nearly allied to them, flesh of their flesh, who inasmuch as the children were made partakers of flesh and blood, he also himself likewise took part of the same (Heb. ii. 14), and is become by special title their authorized Lord, they are assured (of that, than which nothing should be more grateful to them) "they shall be for ever with the Lord ;" that they are to be where he is, "to behold his glory ;" and shall be "joint-heirs with Christ," and be "glorified together with him," shall partake, according to their measure and capacity, in the same blessedness which he enjoys. Thou canst not pretend, sinner, who livest under the gospel, that thou hast not the light of the day to shew thee what blessedness is. Heaven is opened to thee. Glory beams down from thence upon thee to create thee a day, by the light whereof thou mayst see with sufficient clearness what is "the inheritance of the saints in light." And though all be not told thee, and it do not in every respect appear what we shall be ; so much may be fore-known, that when he shall appear, we shall be like him, and shall see him as he is, 1 John iii. 1, 2. And because the heart, as yet carnal, can savour little of all this ; and finding itself strange and disaffected to God, affecting now to be without Christ and without God in the world, may easily apprehend it impossible to it to be happy in an undesired good, or that it can enjoy what it dislikes ; or, in the mean time, walk in a way to which it finds in itself nothing but utter averseness and disinclination.

5. The gospel further shews us what is to be wrought and done in us to attemper and frame our spirits to our future state and present way to it. It lets us know we are to be born again, born from above, born of God, made partakers of a divine nature, that will make the temper of our spirits connatural to the divine presence. That whereas "God is light, and with him is no darkness at all," we "who were darkness shall be made light in the Lord :" that we are to be "begotten again to a lively hope, to the eternal and undefiled inheritance that is reserved in the heavens for us :" that we are thus to be made "meet to

be partakers of that inheritance of the saints in light." And as we are to be eternally conversant with Christ, we are here to put on Christ, to have Christ in us the hope of glory. And whereas only the way of holiness and obedience leads to blessedness, that we are to be " created in Christ Jesus to good works to walk in them." And shall thereupon find the ways prescribed to us by him, who is the Wisdom of God, to be all " ways of pleasantness and paths of peace :" that he will " put his Spirit into us, and cause us to walk in his statutes," and to account that " in keeping them there is great reward." And thus all that is contained in that mentioned summary of the things belonging to our peace, " repentance towards God, and faith in our Lord Jesus Christ," will all become easy to us, and as the acts of nature ; proceeding from that new and holy nature imparted to us.

And whosoever thou art that livest under the gospel, canst thou deny that it is day with thee, as to all this ? Wast thou never told of this great necessary heart-change ? Didst thou never hear that the " tree must be made good that the fruit might be good ?" that thou must become a " new creature, have old things done away, and all things made new ?" Didst thou never hear of the necessity of having " a new heart, and a right spirit" created and renewed in thee ; that except thou wert " born again," or from above (as that expression may be read), thou couldst " never enter into the kingdom of God ?" Wast thou kept in ignorance that a form of godliness without the power of it would never do thee good ? that a name to live without the principle of the holy, divine life, would never save thee ? that a specious outside, that all thy external performances, while thou wentest with an unrenewed, earthly, carnal heart, would never advantage thee as to thy eternal salvation and blessedness ? And this might help thine understanding concerning the nature of thy future blessedness, and will be found most agreeable to it, being aright understood : for as thou art not to be blessed by a blessedness without thee and distant from thee, but inwrought into thy temper, and intimately united with thee, nor glorified by an external glory, but by a glory revealed within thee; so nor canst thou be qualified for that blessed glorious state otherwise than by having the temper of thy soul made habitually holy and good. As what a good man partakes of happiness here is such, that he is " satisfied from himself;" so it must be hereafter, not originally from himself, but by divine communication made most intimate to him. Didst thou not know that it belonged to thy peace, to have a peace-maker? and that the Son of God was he? and that he makes not the peace of those that despise and refuse him, or that receive him not, that come not to him, and are not willing to come to God by him? Couldst thou think, living under the gospel, that the reconciliation between God and thee was not to be mutual? that he would be reconciled to thee while thou wouldst not be reconciled to him, or shouldst still bear towards him a disaffected, implacable heart? For couldst thou be so void of all understanding as not to apprehend what the gospel was sent to thee for? or why it was necessary to be preached to thee, or that thou shouldst hear it? Who was to be reconciled by a gospel preached to thee but thyself? who was to be persuaded by a gospel sent to thee? God, or thou? Who is to be persuaded but the unwilling? The gospel, as thou hast been told, reveals God willing to be reconciled, and thereupon beseeches thee to be reconciled to him. Or could it seem likely to thee thou couldst ever be reconciled to God, and continue unreconciled to thy Reconciler? To what purpose is there a days-man, a middle person between God and thee, if thou wilt not meet him in that middle person? Dost thou not know that Christ avails thee nothing if thou still stand at a distance with him, if thou dost not unite and adjoin thyself to him, or art not in him? And dost thou not again know that divine power and grace must unite thee to him? and that a work must be wrought and done upon thy soul by an Almighty hand, by God himself, a mighty transforming work, to make thee capable of that union? (2 Cor. v. 17) that whosoever is in Christ is a new creature ? (1 Cor. i. 30) that thou must be of God in Christ Jesus, who then is made unto thee of God also wisdom, righteousness, sanctification, and redemption; every way answering the exigency of thy case, as thou art a foolish, guilty, impure, and enslaved, or lost creature ? Didst thou never hear, that none can come to Christ but whom the Father draws ? and that he draws the reasonable souls of men not violently or against their wills (he draws, yet drags them not), but makes them willing in the day of power, by giving a new nature and new inclinations to them ? 'Tis sure with thee not dark night, not a dubious twilight, but broad day as to all this.

Yes, perhaps thou mayst say, but this makes my case the worse, not the better ; for it gives me at length to understand that what is necessary to my peace and welfare is impossible to me ; and so the light of my day doth but serve to let me see myself miserable and undone, and that I have nothing to do to relieve and help myself. I therefore add,

6. That by being under the gospel, men nave not only light to understand whatsoever is any way necessary to their peace, but opportunity to obtain that communication of divine power and grace whereby to comply with the terms of it. Whereupon, if this be made good, you have not a pretence left you to say your case is the worse, or that you receive any prejudice by what the gospel reveals of your own impotency to relieve and help yourselves ; or determines touching the terms of your peace and salvation, making such things necessary thereto, as are to you impossible, and out of your own present power, unless it be a prejudice to you not to have your pride gratified ; and that God hath pitched upon such a method for your salvation, as shall wholly turn to the praise of the glory of his grace, or that you are to be *of him* (1 Cor. i. 30, 31) in Christ Jesus—that whosoever glories might glory in the Lord. Is it for a sinner that hath deserved, and is ready to perish, to insist upon being saved with reputation ? or to envy the

great God, upon whose pleasure it wholly depends whether
he shall be saved or not saved, the entire glory of saving
him ? For otherwise, excepting the mere business of glory
and reputation ; is it not all one to you whether you have
the power in your own hands of changing your hearts, of
being the authors to yourselves of that holy, new nature,
out of which actual faith and repentance are to spring, or
whether you may have it from the God of all grace, flowing
to you from its own proper divine fountain ? Your case is not
sure really the worse that your salvation from first to last
is to be all of grace, and that it is impossible to you to repent and believe, while it is not simply impossible ; but
that he can effectually enable you thereto, unto whom all
things are possible ; supposing that he will : whereof by
and by. Nay, and it is more glorious and honourable, even
to you, if you understand yourselves, that your case is so
stated as it is. The gospel indeed plainly tells you that
your repentance must be given you. Christ " is exalted
to be a Prince and a Saviour, to give repentance and remission of sins." And so must your faith, and that frame
of spirit which is the principle of all good works. By grace
ye are saved, through faith, not of yourselves, it is the gift
of God : not of works, lest any man should boast ; for we
are his workmanship, created in Christ Jesus unto good
works, which God hath before ordained that we should
walk in them, Ephes. ii. 8–10. Is it more glorious to
have nothing in you but what is self-sprung, than to have
your souls the seat and receptacle of divine communica-
tions ; of so excellent things as could have no other than
a heavenly original ? If it were not absurd and impossible you should be self-begotten, is it not much more
glorious to be born of God ? As they are said to be that
receive Christ, John i. 12, 13. But as many as received
him, to them gave he power to become the sons of God,
even to them that believe on his name : which were born,
not of blood, nor of the will of the flesh, nor of the will of
man, but of God.

And now that, by being under the gospel, you have the

opportunity of getting that grace, which is necessary to your peace and salvation ; you may see, if you consider what the gospel is, and was designed for. It is the ministration of the Spirit ; that Spirit by which you are to be born again, John iii. 3, 5, 6. The work of regeneration consists in the impregnating, and making lively and efficacious, in you the holy truths contained in the gospel. Of his own good will begat he us with the word of truth, that we should be a kind of first-fruits of his creatures, James i. 18. And again, being born again, not of corruptible seed, but of incorruptible, by the word of God, 1 Pet. i. 23. So our Saviour prays : Sanctify them through thy truth, thy word is truth, John xvii. 17. The gospel is, upon this account, called the word of life, Phil. ii. 16, as by which the principles of that divine and holy life are implanted in the soul, whereby we live to God, do what his gospel requires, and hath made our duty, and that ends at length in eternal life. But you will say, Shall all, then, that live under the gospel obtain this grace and holy life ? Or if they shall not, or, if so far as can be collected, multitudes do not, or, perhaps, in some places that enjoy the gospel, very few do, in comparison of them that do not, what am I better ? when, perhaps, it is far more likely that I shall perish notwithstanding, than be saved ? In answer to this, it must be acknowledged, that all that live under the gospel do not obtain life and saving grace by it. For then there had been no occasion for this lamentation of our blessed Lord over the perishing inhabitants of Jerusalem, as having lost their day, and that the things of their peace were now hid from their eyes ; and by that instance it appears too possible, that even the generality of a people living under the gospel may fall at length into the like forlorn and hopeless condition. But art thou a man that thus objectest ? A reasonable understanding creature ? Or dost thou use the reason and understanding of a man in objecting thus ? Didst thou expect, that when thine own wilful transgression had made thee liable to eternal death and wrath, peace, and life, and salvation should be imposed upon thee whether

thou wouldst or no, or notwithstanding thy most wilful
neglect and contempt of them, and all the means of them ?
Could it enter into thy mind, that a reasonable soul should
be wrought and framed for that high and blessed end,
whereof it is radically capable, as a stock or a stone is for
any use it is designed for, without designing its own end
or way to it ? Couldst thou think the gospel was to bring
thee to faith and repentance, whether thou didst hear it or
no ? or ever apply thy mind to consider the meaning of it,
and what it did propose and offer to thee ? or when thou
mightest so easily understand that the grace of God was
necessary to make it effectual to thee, and that it might
become his power (or the instrument of his power) to thy
salvation, couldst thou think it concerned thee not to sue
and supplicate to him for that grace, when thy life lay
upon it, and thy eternal hope ? Hast thou lain weltering
at the footstool of the throne of grace in thine own tears
(as thou hast been formerly weltering in thy sins and im-
purities), crying for grace to help thee in this time of thy
need ? And if thou thinkest this was above thee and without thy compass, hast thou done all that was within thy
compass in order to the obtaining of grace at God's hands ?
But here, perhaps, thou wilt inquire, Is there any thing,
then, to be done by us whereupon the grace of God may
be expected certainly to follow ? To which I answer,

1. That it is out of question nothing can be done by us
to deserve it, or *for which* we may expect it to follow. It
were not grace if we had obliged, or brought it, by our
desert, under former preventive bonds to us. And,

2. What if nothing can be done by us *upon which* it may
be *certainly* expected to follow ? Is a certainty of perishing better than a high probability of being saved ?

3. Such as live under the gospel have reason to apprehend it highly probable they may obtain that grace which
is necessary to their salvation, if they be not wanting to
themselves. For,

4. There is generally afforded to such that which is
wont to be called common grace. I speak not of any

further extent of it, 'tis enough to our present purpose that it extends so far, as to them that live under the gospel, and have thereby a day allowed them wherein to provide for their peace. Now, though this grace is not yet certainly saving, yet it tends to that which is so. And none have cause to despair, but that being duly improved and complied with, it may end in it.

And this is that which requires to be insisted on, and more fully evinced. In order whereto let it be considered, that it is expressly said to such, they are to work out their salvation with fear and trembling, for this reason, that God works (or is working ἔστιν ὁ ἐνεργῶν) in them, i. e., statedly and continually at work, or is always ready to work in them, to will and to do of his own good pleasure, Phil. ii. 12, 13. The matter fails not on his part. He will work on in order to their salvation, if they work in that way of subordinate co-operation, which his command, and the necessity of their own case, oblige them unto. And it is further to be considered, that where God had formerly afforded the symbols of his gracious presence, given his oracles, and settled his church, though yet in its nonage, and much more imperfect state, there he, however, communicated those influences of his Spirit, that it was to be imputed to themselves if they came short of the saving operations of it. Of such it was said, Thou gavest thy good Spirit to instruct them, Nehem. ix. 20. And to such, Turn ye at my reproof, I will pour out my Spirit unto you, I will make known my words unto you. Because I called and you refused, I stretched out my hand and no man regarded, but ye set at nought my counsel, and despised all my reproof, I also will laugh at your calamity, &c., Prov. i. 23, 24. We see whence their destruction came ; not from God's first restraint of his Spirit, but their refusing, despising, and setting at nought his counsels and reproofs. And when it is said, they rebelled and vexed his Spirit, and he therefore turned and fought against them, and became their enemy, Isa. lxiii. 10, it appears, that before his Spirit was not withheld, but did variously, and often, make essays and attempts upon them. And when Stephen, immediately before his martyrdom, thus bespeaks the descendants of these Jews, Ye stiff-necked, and uncircumcised,—ye do always resist the Holy Ghost, as your fathers did, so do ye, Acts vii., 'tis implied the Holy Ghost had been always striving from age to age with that stubborn people : for where there is no counter-striving there can be no resistance, no more than there can be a war on one side only. Which also appears to have been the course of God's dealing with the old world, before their so general lapse into idolatry and sensual wickedness, from that passage, Gen. vi. 3, according to the more common reading and sense of those words.

Now whereas the gospel is eminently said to be the ministration of the Spirit in contradistinction not only to the natural religion of other nations, but the divinely instituted religion of the Jews also, as is largely discoursed, 2 Cor. iii., and more largely through the Epistle to the Galatians, especially chap. iv. ; and whereas we find that, in the Jewish church, the Holy Ghost did generally diffuse its influences, and not otherwise withhold them, than penally, and upon great provocation ; how much more may it be concluded, that under the gospel, the same blessed Spirit is very generally at work upon the souls of men, till by their resisting, grieving, and quenching of it, they provoke it to retire and withdraw from them.

And let the consciences of men living under the gospel testify in the case. Appeal sinner to thine own conscience ; Hast thou never felt any thing of conviction, by the word of God ? hadst thou never any thought injected of turning to God, of reforming thy life, of making thy peace ? have no desires ever been raised in thee, no fears ? hast thou never had any tastes and relishes of pleasure in the things of God ? whence have these come ? What ! from thyself, who art not sufficient to think any thing as of thyself ? *i. e.* not any good or right thought. All must be from that good Spirit that hath been striving with thee ; and might still have been so unto a blessed issue for thy soul, if thou hadst not neglected and disobeyed it.

And do not go about to excuse thyself by saying, that so all others have done too, 'tis like, at one time or other; and if that therefore be the rule and measure, that they that contend against the strivings and motions of God's Spirit must be finally deserted and given up to perish, who then can be saved? Think not of pleading so for thy neglecting and despising the grace and Spirit of God. 'Tis true that herein the great God shews his sovereignty: when all that enjoy the same advantages for salvation deserve by their slighting them to be forsaken alike; he gives instances and makes examples of just severity, and of the victorious power of grace, as seems him good, which there will be further occasion to speak more of hereafter. In the mean time the present design is not to justify thy condemnation but procure thy salvation, and therefore to admonish and instruct thee, that, though thou art not sure, because some others that have slighted and despised the grace and Spirit of God are notwithstanding conquered and saved thereby, it shall therefore fare as well with thee; yet thou hast reason to be confident, it will be well and happy for thee, if now thou despise and slight them not. And whether thou do or not, it is however plain, that by being under the gospel thou hast had a day, wherein to mind the things of thy peace, though it is not told thee it would last always, but the contrary is presently to be told thee.

And thou mayst now see 'tis not only a day in respect of *light* but *influence* also; that thou mightest not only know notionally what belonged thereto, but efficaciously and practically; which you have heard is the knowledge here meant. And the concurrence of such light and influence has made thee a season wherein thou wast to have been at work for thy soul. The day is the proper season for work: when the night comes working ceases, both because that then light fails, and because drowsiness and sloth are more apt to possess men. And the night will come. For (which is the next thing we have to speak to),

III. This day hath its bounds and limits, so that when it is over and lost with such, the things of their peace are for ever hid from their eyes. And that this day is not infinite and endless, we see in the present instance. Jerusalem had her day; but that day had its period, we see it comes to this at last, that *now* the things of her peace are hid from her eyes. We generally see the same thing, in that sinners are so earnestly pressed to make use of the present time. To-day if you will hear his voice, harden not your hearts, Psal. xcv, quoted and urged Heb. iii. 7, 8. They are admonished to seek the Lord while he may be found, to call upon him while he is nigh, Isa. lv. It seems some time he will not be found, and will be afar off. They are told this is the accepted time, this is the day of salvation, Isa. xlix.; 2 Cor. vi.

This day, with any place or people, supposes a precedent night, when the day-spring from on high had not visited their horizon, and all within it sat in darkness, and in the region and shadow of death. Yea, and there was a time, we know, of very general darkness, when the gospel day, " the day of visitation," had not yet dawned upon the world; " times of ignorance," wherein God as it were winked upon the nations of the earth; the beams of his eye did in a sort overshoot them, as the word ὑπεριδὼν imports. But when the eyelids of the morning open upon any people, and light shines to them with direct beams, they are *now* commanded to repent (Acts, xvii. 30), limited to the present point of time with such peremptoriness, as that noble Roman used towards a proud prince, asking time to deliberate upon the proposal made to him of withdrawing his forces that molested some of the allies of that state; he draws a line about him with the end of his rod, and requires him now, out of hand, before he stirred out of that circle, to make his choice, whether he would be a friend or enemy to the people of Rome. So are sinners to understand the state of their own case. The God of thy life, sinner, in whose hands thy times are, doth with much **higher right limit thee to the present time, and expects** thy present answer to his just and merciful offers and demands. He circumscribes thy day of grace ; it is enclosed on both parts, and hath an evening as well as morning ; as it had a foregoing, so hath it a subsequent night, and the latter, if not more dark, yet usually much more stormy than the former ! For God shuts up this day in much displeasure, which hath terrible effects. If it be not expressly told you what the condition of that night is that follows your gospel day ; if the watchman being asked, " What of the night ?" do only answer it cometh as well as the morning came ; black events are signified by that more awful silence. Or, 'tis all one if you call it *a day ;* there is enough to distinguish it from the *day of grace.* The Scriptures call such a calamitous season indifferently either by the name of night or day ; but the latter name is used with some or other adjunct, to signify *day* is not meant in the pleasant or more grateful sense : a day of wrath, an evil day, a day of gloominess and thick darkness, not differing from the most dismal night ; and to be told the morning of such a day is coming, is all one, as that the evening is coming of a bright and a serene day.

And here perhaps, reader, thou will expect to be told what are the limits of this day of grace. It is indeed much more difficult punctually to assign those limits, than to ascertain thee there are such ; but it is also less necessary. The wise and merciful God doth in matters of this nature little mind to gratify our curiosity ; much less is it to be expected from him, that he should make known to us such things, whereof it were better we were ignorant, or the knowledge whereof would be much more a prejudice to us than an advantage. And it were as bold and rash an undertaking, in this case, as it would be vain and insignificant, for any man to take on him to say, in it, what God hath not said, or given him plain ground for. What I conceive to be plain and useful in this matter I shall lay down in the following propositions, insisting more largely where the matter requires it, and contenting myself but to mention what is obvious, and clear at the first sight.

1. That there is a great difference between the ends and limits of the day or season of grace as to particular persons, and in reference to the collective body of a people, inhabiting this or that place. It may be over with such or such a place, so as that they that dwell there shall no longer have the gospel among them, when as yet it may not be over with every particular person belonging to it, who may be providentially cast elsewhere, or may have the "ingrafted word" in them, which they lose not. And again, it may be over with some particular persons in such a place, when it is not yet over with that people or place, generally considered.

2. As to both there is a difference between the ending of such a day, and intermissions, or dark intervals, that may be in it. The gospel may be withdrawn from such a people, and be restored. And God often, no doubt, as to particular persons, either deprives them of the outward means of grace for a time (by sickness, or many other ways), or may for a time forbear moving upon them by his Spirit, and again try them with both.

3. As to particular persons, there may be much difference between such as, while they lived under the gospel, gained the knowledge of the principal doctrines, or of the sum or substance, of Christianity, though without any sanctifying effect or impression upon their hearts, and such as, through their own negligence, lived under it in total ignorance hereof. The day of grace may not be over with the former, though they should never live under the ministry of the gospel more. For it is possible, while they have the seeds and principles of holy truth laid up in their minds, God may graciously administer to them many occasions of recollecting and considering them, wherewith he may so please to co-operate, as to enliven them, and make them vital and effectual to their final salvation. Whereas, with the other sort, when they no more enjoy the external means, the day of grace is like to be quite over, so as that there may be no more hope in their case than in that of pagans in the darkest parts of the world ; and perhaps much less,

as their guilt hath been much greater by their neglect of so great and important things. It may be better with Tyre and Sidon, &c.

4. That yet it is a terrible judgment to the most knowing, to lose the external dispensation of the gospel, while they have yet no sanctifying impression upon their hearts by it, and they are cast upon a fearful hazard of being lost for ever, being left by the departed gospel in an unconverted state. For they need the most urgent inculcations of gospel truths, and the most powerful enforcing means, to engage them to consider the things which they know. It is the design of the gospel to beget not only light in the mind, but grace in the heart. And if that were not done while they enjoyed such means, it is less likely to be done without them. And if any slighter and more superficial impressions were made upon them thereby, short of true and thorough conversion, how great is the danger that all will vanish, when they cease to be pressed and urged, and called upon by the public voice of the gospel-ministry any more. How naturally desident is the spirit of man, and apt to sink into deadness, worldliness, and carnality, even under the most lively and quickening means; and even where a saving work hath been wrought! how much more when those means fail, and there is no vital principle within, capable of self-excitation and improvement! O that they would consider this, who have got nothing by the gospel all this while, but a little cold, spiritless, notional, knowledge, and are in a possibility of losing it before they get any thing more!

5. That as it is certain, death ends the day of grace with every unconverted person, so it is very possible it may end with divers before they die; by their total loss of all external means, or by the departure of the blessed Spirit of God from them, so as to return and visit them no more. How the day of grace may end with a person, is to be understood by considering what it is that makes up and constitutes such a day. There must be some measure and

proportion of time to make up this (or any) day, which is as the *substratum* and ground forelaid. Then there must be light superadded, otherwise it differs not from night, which may have the same measure of mere time. The gospel-revelation some way or other must be had, as being the light of such a day. And again there must be some degree of liveliness, and vital influence, the more usual concomitant of light ; the night doth more dispose men to drowsiness. The same sun that enlightens the world, disseminates also an invigorating influence. If the Spirit of the living God do no way animate the gospel-revelation, and breathe in it, we have no day of grace. It is not only a day of light, but a day of power, wherein souls can be wrought upon, and a people made willing to become the Lord's, Psal. cx. As the Redeemer revealed in the gospel is the light of the world, so he is life to it too, though neither are planted or do take root every where. In him was life, and that life was the light of men. That light that rays from him is vital light in itself, and in its tendency and design, though it be disliked and not entertained by the most.

Whereas therefore these things must concur to make up such a day : if either a man's time, his life on earth, expire, or if light quite fail him, or if all gracious influence be withheld, so as to be communicated no more ; his day is done, the season of grace is over with him. Now it is plain, that many a one may lose the gospel before his life end ; and possible that all gracious influence may be restrained, while as yet the external dispensation of the gospel remains. A sinner may have hardened his heart to that degree, that God will attempt him no more, in any kind, with any design of kindness to him, not in that more inward, immediate way at all, *i. e.* by the motions of his Spirit, which peculiarly can import nothing but friendly inclination, as whereby men are personally applied unto, so that cannot be meant ; nor by the voice of the gospel, which may either be continued for the sake of others, or they continued under it, but for their heavier doom at length. Which though it may seem severe, is not to be thought strange, much less unrighteous.

It is not to be thought strange to them that read the Bible, which so often speaks this sense : as when it warns and threatens men with so much terror, as Heb. x. 26–29. For if we sin wilfully after that we have received the knowledge of the truth, there remaineth no more sacrifice for sins, but a fearful looking for of judgment, and fiery indignation, which shall devour the adversaries. He that despised Moses' law, died without mercy, under two or three witnesses : of how much sorer punishment, suppose ye, shall he be thought worthy, who hath trodden under foot the Son of God, and hath counted the blood of the covenant, wherewith he was sanctified, an unholy thing, and hath *done despite unto the Spirit of grace ?* And when it tells us, after many overtures made to men in vain, of his having given them up, &c. Psal. lxxxi. 11, 12. But my people would not hearken to my voice ; and Israel would none of me ; so I gave them up unto their own heart's lust ; and they walked in their own counsels : and pronounces, Let him that is unjust, be unjust still, and let him which is filthy, be filthy still, Rev. xxii. 11, and says, In thy filthiness is lewdness, because I have purged thee and thou wast not purged ; thou shalt not be purged from thy filthiness any more, till I have caused my fury to rest upon thee, Ezek. xxiv. 13. Which passages seem to imply a total desertion of them, and retraction of all gracious influence. And when it speaks of letting them be under the gospel, and the ordinary means of salvation, for the most direful purposes : as that, This child (Jesus) was set for the fall, as well as for the rising, of many in Israel, Luke, ii. 34. As to which text the very learned Grotius, glossing upon the words κεῖται and εἰς πτῶσιν, says, *Accedo iis qui non necdum eventum, sed et consilium,* that *he is of their opinion who think not that the naked event, but the counsel or purpose of God, is signified by it, the same with* τίθεται ; and alleges several texts where the active of that verb must have the same sense, as to appoint or ordain ;

and mentions divers other places of the same import with this so understood ; and which therefore to recite will equally serve our present purpose ; as that, Rom. ix. 33. Behold, I lay in Zion a stumbling stone, and rock of offence. And 1 Pet. ii. 8. The stone which the builders refused, is made a stone of stumbling, and a rock of offence, even to them which stumble at the word, being disobedient, whereunto also they were appointed. With that of our Saviour himself, John, ix. 39. For judgment I am come into this world, that they which see not might see ; and that they which see, might be made blind. And most agreeable to those former places is that of the prophet Isaiah, xxviii. 13. But the word of the Lord was unto them precept upon precept, precept upon precept, line upon line, line upon line, here a little and there a little ; that they might go, and fall backward, and be broken, and snared, and taken. And we may add, that our Lord hath put us out of doubt that there is such a sin as that which is eminently called the sin against the Holy Ghost ; that a man may, in such circumstances, and to such a degree, sin against that blessed Spirit, that he will never move or breathe upon them more, but leave them to a hopeless ruin ; though I shall not in this discourse determine or discuss the nature of it. But I doubt not it is somewhat else than final impenitency and infidelity ; and that every one that dies, not having sincerely repented and believed, is not guilty of it, though every one that is guilty of it, dies impenitent and unbelieving, but was guilty of it before ; so as it is not the mere want of time, that makes him guilty. Whereupon therefore, that such may outlive their day of grace, is out of question.

But let not such, as, upon the descriptions the gospel gives us of that sin, may be justly confident they have not perhaps committed it, therefore think themselves out of danger of losing their season of making their peace with God before they die. Many a one may, no doubt, that never committed the unpardonable blasphemy against the Holy Ghost, as he is the witness, by his wonderful works, of Christ being the Messiah. As one may die, by neglect-ing himself, that doth not poison himself, or cut his own throat. You will say, " But if the Spirit retire from men, so as never to return, where is the difference ?" I answer, the difference lies in the *specific nature* and greater heinous-ness of that sin, and consequently, in the deeper degrees of its punishment. For though the reason of its unpardon-ableness lies not principally in its greater heinousness, but in its direct repugnancy to the way of obtaining par-don, yet there is no doubt of its being much more heinous than many other sins for which men perish. And there-fore 'tis in proportion more severely punished. But is it not misery enough to dwell in darkness and woe for ever, as every one that dies unreconciled to God must do, unless the most intense flames and horror of hell be your portion? As his case is sufficiently bad that must die as an ordinary felon, though he is not to be hanged, drawn, and quartered.

Nor is there any place or pretence for so profane a thought, as if there were any colour of unrighteousness in this course of procedure with such men. Is it unjust severity to let the gospel become deadly to them whose malignity perverts it, against its nature, and genuine tendency, into a savour of death (as 2 Cor. ii. 16), which it is τοῖς ἀπολλυμένοις, *i. e.* to them (as the mentioned author speaks) who may be truly said to seek their own destruction? or that God should intend their more aggravated condemnation, even from the despised gospel itself, who, when such light is come into the world, hate it, shew them-selves *lucifugæ, tenebriones* (as he also phrases it, speaking further upon that first mentioned text), *such as fly from the light, choose and love to lurk in darkness ?* He must have very low thoughts of divine favour and acceptance, of Christ, and grace, and glory, that can have hard thoughts of God, for his vindicating, with greatest severity, the contempt of such things. What could better become his glorious majesty, and excellent greatness, than, as all things work together for good towards them that love him, so to let all things work for the hurt of them that so irreconcilably hate him, and bear a disaffected and implacable mind towards him? Nor doth the addition of his designing the matter so, make it hard. For if it be just to punish such wickedness, is it unjust to intend to punish it? and to intend to punish it according to its desert, when it cannot be thought unjust actually to render to men what they deserve?

We are, indeed, to account the primary intention of continuing the gospel to such a people, among whom these live, is kindness towards others, not this higher revenge upon them; yet nothing hinders but that this revenge upon them, may also be the fit matter of his secondary intention. For should he intend nothing concerning them? Is he to be so unconcerned about his own creatures that are under his government? While things cannot fall out to him unawares, but that he hath this dismal event in prospect before him, he must at least intend to let it be, or not to hinder it. And who can expect he should? For, that his gracious influence towards them should at length cease, is above all exception: that it ceasing, while they live still under the gospel, they contract deeper guilt, and incur heavier punishment, follows of course. And who can say he should not intend to let it follow? For should he take away the gospel from the rest, that these might be less punished? that others might not be saved, because they will not?

Nor can he be obliged to interpose extraordinarily, and alter for their sakes the course of nature and providence, so as either to hasten them the sooner out of the world, or cast them into any other part of it, where the gospel is not, lest they should, by living still under it, be obnoxious to the severer punishment. For whither would this lead? He should, by equal reason, have been obliged to prevent men's sinning at all, that they might not be liable to any punishment. And so not to have made the world, or have otherwise framed the methods of his government, and less suitably to a whole community of reasonable creatures; or to have made an end of the world long ago, and have quitted all his great designs in it, lest some should sin on, and incur proportionable punishment ! or to have provided extraordinarily that all should do and fare alike ; and that it might never have come to pass, that it should be less tolerable for Capernaum, and Chorazin, and Bethsaida, than for Tyre, and Sidon, and Sodom, and Gomorrah. But is there unrighteousness with God ? or is he unrighteous in taking vengeance ? or is he therefore unjust, because he will render to every one according to his works ; to them who, by patient continuance in well doing, seek glory, honour, and immortality, eternal life ; but unto them that are contentious, and do not obey the truth, but obey unrighteousness, indignation and wrath, tribulation and anguish upon every soul of man that doth evil, of the Jew first, and also of the Gentile ? Rom. ii. 6–9. Doth righteousness itself make him unrighteous ? O sinner, understand how much better it is to avoid the stroke of divine justice than accuse it ! God will be found true, and every man a liar, that he may be justified when he speaks, and be clear when he judges, Psal. li. 4.

6. Yet are we not to imagine any certain fixed rule, according whereto (except in the case of the unpardonable sin) the divine dispensation is measured in cases of this nature : viz. That, when a sinner hath contended just so long, or to such a degree, against his grace and Spirit in his gospel, he shall be finally rejected ; or if but so long, or not to such a degree, he is yet certainly to be further tried, or treated with. It is little to be doubted, but he puts forth the power of victorious grace, at length, upon some more obstinate and obdurate sinners, and that have longer persisted in their rebellions (not having sinned the unpardonable sin), and gives over some sooner, as it seems good unto him. Nor doth he herein owe an account to any man of his matters. Here sovereign good pleasure rules and arbitrates, that is tied to no certain rule. Neither, in these variations, is there any shew of that blameable προσωπολη$ψ$ία or *accepting of persons*, which, in his own word, he so expressly disclaims. We must distinguish matters of right (even such as are so by promise only, as

well as others), and matters of mere unpromised favour. In matters of right, to be an accepter of persons, is a thing most highly culpable with men, and which can have no place with the holy God : *i. e.* when a human judge hath his rule before him, according whereto he is to estimate men's rights, in judgment ; there, to regard the person of the rich, or of the poor, to the prejudice of the justice of the cause, were an insufferable iniquity ; as it were also in a private person to withhold another's right, because he hath no kindness for him. So even the great God himself, though of mere grace he first fixed and established the rule (fitly therefore called the covenant, or law of grace), by which he will proceed in pardoning and justifying men, or in condemning and holding them guilty, both here and in the final judgment ; yet having fixed it, he will never recede from it ; so as either to acquit an impenitent unbeliever, or condemn a believing penitent. If we confess our sins, he is faithful and just to forgive. None shall be ever able to accuse him of breach of faith, or of transgressing his own rules of justice. We find it therefore said in reference to the judgment of the last day, when God shall render to every man according to his works, whether they be Jews or Gentiles, that there is no respect of persons with God, Rom. ii. 6–11, yet (*qui promisit pœnitenti veniam, non promisit peccanti pœnitentiam*) whereas he hath, by his evangelical law, ascertained pardon to one that sincerely obeys it, but hath not promised grace to enable them to do so, to them that have long continued wilfully disobedient and rebellious ; this communication of grace is, therefore, left arbitrary, and to be dispensed, as the matter of free and unassured favour, as it seems him good. And indeed, if in matters of arbitrary favour, respect of persons ought to have no place, friendship were quite excluded the world, and would be swallowed up of strict and rigid justice. I ought to take all men for my friends alike, otherwise than as justice should oblige me to be more respectful to men of more merit.

7. Wherefore no man can certainly know, or ought to

conclude, concerning himself or others, as long as they live, that the season of grace is quite over with them. As we can conceive no rule God hath set to himself to proceed by, in ordinary cases of this nature ; so nor is there any he hath set unto us to judge by, in this case. It were to no purpose, and could be of no use to men, to know so much ; therefore it were unreasonable to expect God should have settled and declared any rule, by which they might come by the knowledge of it. As the case is then, viz. there being no such rule, no such thing can be concluded ; for who can tell what an arbitrary, sovereign, free agent will do, if he declare not his own purpose himself ? How should it be known, when the Spirit of God hath been often working upon the soul of a man, that this or that shall be the last act, and that he will never put forth another ? And why should God make it known ? To the person himself whose case it is, 'tis manifest it could be no benefit. Nor is it to be thought the holy God will ever so alter the course of his own proceedings, but that it shall finally be seen to all the world, that every man's destruction was, entirely, and to the last, of himself. If God had made it evident to a man, that he were finally rejected, he were obliged to believe it. But shall it ever be said, God hath made any thing a man's duty, which were inconsistent with his felicity. The having sinned himself into such a condition wherein he is forsaken of God, is indeed inconsistent with it. And so the case is to stand, *i.e.* that his perdition be in immediate connexion with his sin, not with his duty. As it would be in immediate, necessary connexion with his duty, if he were bound to believe himself finally forsaken, and a lost creature. For that belief makes him hopeless, and a very devil, justifies his unbelief of the gospel, towards himself, by removing and shutting up, towards him, the object of such a faith, and consequently brings the matter to this state, that he perishes,* not because he doth not believe God

* See more to this purpose in the Appendix.

reconcilable to man, but because, with particular application to himself, he ought not so to believe.

And it were most unfit, and of very pernicious consequence, that such a thing should be generally known concerning others. It were to anticipate the final judgment, to create a hell upon earth, to tempt them whose doom were already known, to do all the mischief in the world, which malice and despair can suggest, and prompt them unto ; it were to mingle devils with men ! and fill the world with confusion ! How should parents know how to behave themselves towards children, a husband towards the wife of his bosom in such a case, if it were known they were no more to counsel, exhort, admonish them, pray with or for them, than if they were devils !

And if there were such a rule, how frequent misapplications would the fallible and distempered minds of men make of it ! so that they would be apt to fancy themselves warranted to judge severely, or uncharitably, and (as the truth of the case perhaps is) unjustly concerning others, from which they are so hardly withheld, when they have no such pretence to embolden them to it, but are so strictly forbidden it ; and the judgment-seat so fenced, as it is, by the most awful interdicts against their usurpations and encroachments. We are therefore to reverence the wisdom of the divine government, that things of this nature are among the arcana of it ; some of those secrets which belong not to us. He hath revealed what was fit and necessary for us and our children, and envies to man no useful knowledge.

But it may be said, when the apostle (1 John, v. 16) directs to pray for a brother whom we see sinning a sin that is not unto death, and adds, there is a sin unto death, I do not say he shall pray for it ; is it not implied that it may be known when one sins that sin unto death, not only to himself, but even to others too ? I answer, it is implied there may be too probable appearances of it, and much ground to suspect and fear it concerning some, in some cases ; as when any against the highest evidence of the truth of the Christian religion, and that Jesus is the Christ, or the Messiah (the proper and most sufficiently credible testimony whereof, he had mentioned in the foregoing verses, under heads to which the whole evidence of the truth of Christianity may be fitly enough reduced), do notwithstanding, from that malice which blinds their understanding, persist in infidelity, or apostatize and relapse into it from a former profession, there is great cause of suspicion, lest such have sinned that sin unto death. Whereupon yet it is to be observed, he doth not expressly forbid praying for the persons whose case we may doubt ; only he doth not enjoin it, as he doth for others, but only says, I do not say ye shall pray for it, *i. e.* that in his present direction to pray for others, he did not intend such, but another sort, for whom they might pray remotely from any such suspicion : viz. that he meant *now* such praying as ought to be interchanged between Christian friends, that have reason, in the main, to be well persuaded concerning one another. In the mean time intending no opposition to what is elsewhere enjoined, the praying for all men (1 Tim. ii. 1), without the personal exclusion of any, as also our Lord himself prayed indefinitely for his most malicious enemies, Father, forgive them, they know not what they do ; though he had formerly said, there was such a sin as should never be forgiven ; whereof 'tis highly probable some of them were guilty : yet such he doth not expressly except ; but his prayer being in the indefinite, not the universal, form, 'tis to be supposed it must mean such as were within the compass and reach of prayer, and capable of benefit by it. Nor doth the apostle here direct personally to exclude any, only that indefinitely and in the general such must be supposed not meant as had sinned the sin unto death ; or must be conditionally excluded if they had, without determining who had or had not. To which purpose it is very observable, that a more abstract form of expression is used in this latter clause of this verse. For whereas in the former *positive part* of the direction,

he enjoins praying for him or them that had not sinned
unto death (*viz.* concerning whom there was no ground for
any such imagination or suspicion that they had) ; in the
negative part, concerning such as might have sinned it, he
doth not say for him or them, but for it (*i. e.* concerning,
in reference to it), as if he had said, the case in general
only is to be excepted, and if persons are to be distinguished
(since every sin is some one's sin, the sin of some person or
other), let God distinguish, but do not you, 'tis enough for
you to except the sin, committed by whomsoever.   And
though the former part of the verse speaks of a particular
person, " If a man see his brother sin a sin that is not unto
death," which is as determinate to a person as the sight of
our eye can be, it doth not follow the latter part must
suppose a like particular determination of any person's case,
that he hath sinned it.   I may have great reason to be
confident such and such have not, when I can only suspect
that such a one hath.   And it is a thing much less unlikely to be certain to oneself than another, for they that
have sinned unto death, are no doubt so blinded and stupified by it, that they are not more apt or competent to
observe themselves, and consider their case, than others
may be.

8. But though none ought to conclude that their day or
season of grace is quite expired, yet they ought deeply to
apprehend the danger, lest it should expire before their
necessary work be done, and their peace made. For though
it can be of no use to them to know the former, and therefore they have no means appointed them by which to know
it, 'tis of great use to apprehend the latter ; and they have
sufficient ground for the apprehension.   All the cautions
and warnings wherewith the Holy Scripture abounds, of
the kind with those already mentioned, have that manifest
design.   And nothing can be more important, or apposite
to this purpose, than that solemn charge of the great apostle
(Phil. ii. 12), Work out your own salvation with fear and
trembling ; considered together with the subjoined ground
of it, ver. 13, For it is God that worketh in you to will

and to do of his own good pleasure. How correspondent is the one with the other ; *work*, for *he works :* there were no working at all to any purpose, or with any hope, if he did not work. And work with fear and trembling, for he works of his own good pleasure, *q. d.* " 'Twere the greatest folly imaginable to trifle with one that works at so perfect liberty, under no obligation, that may desist when he will ; to impose upon so absolutely sovereign and arbitrary an agent, that owes you nothing ; and from whose former gracious operations not complied with, you can draw no argument unto any following ones, that because he doth, therefore he will. As there is no certain connexion between present time and future, but all time is made up of undepending, not strictly coherent, moments, so as no man can be sure, because one now exists, another shall ; there is also no more certain connexion between the arbitrary acts of a free agent within such time ; so that I cannot be sure, because he now darts in light upon me, is now convincing me, now awakening me, therefore he will still do so, again and again. Upon this ground, then, what exhortation could be more proper than this ? " Work out your salvation with fear and trembling." What could be more awfully monitory, and enforcing of it, than that he works only of mere good will and pleasure ? How should I tremble to think, if I should be negligent, or undutiful, he may give out the next moment, nay let the work fall, and me perish ! And there is more especial cause for such an apprehension, upon the concurrence of such things as these :—

1. If the workings of God's Spirit upon the soul of a man have been more than ordinarily strong and urgent, and do now cease : if there have been more powerful convictions, deeper humiliations, more awakened fears, more formed purposes of a new life, more fervent desires, that are now all vanished and fled, and the sinner is returned to his old dead and dull temper.

2. If there be no disposition to reflect and consider the difference, no sense of his loss, but he apprehends such

workings of spirit in him unnecessary troubles to him, and thinks it well he is delivered and eased of them.

3. If in the time when he was under such workings of spirit, he had made known his case to his minister, or any godly friend, whose company he now shuns, as not willing to be put in mind or hear any more of such matters.

4. If hereupon he hath more indulged sensual inclination, taken more liberty, gone against the checks of his own conscience, broken former good resolutions, involved himself in the guilt of any grosser sins.

5. If conscience, so baffled, be now silent; lets him alone, grows more sluggish and weaker (which it must) as his lusts grow stronger.

6. If the same lively powerful ministry, which before affected him much, now moves him not.

7. If especially he is grown into a dislike of such preaching ; if serious godliness, and what tends to it, are become distasteful to him ; if discourses of God, and Christ, of death and judgment, and of a holy life, are reckoned superfluous and needless, are unsavoury and disrelished ; if he have learned to put disgraceful names upon things of this import, and the persons that most value them, and live accordingly ; if he hath taken the seat of the scorner, and makes it his business to deride what he had once a reverence for, or took some complacency in.

8. If, upon all this, God withdraw such a ministry, so that he is now warned and admonished, exhorted and striven with, as formerly, no more. O the fearful danger of that man's case ! Hath he no cause to fear lest the things of his peace should be for ever hid from his eyes ? Surely he hath much cause of fear, but not of despair. Fear would in this case be his great duty, and might yet prove the means of saving him ; despair would be his very heinous and destroying sin. If yet he would be stirred up to consider his case, whence he is fallen, and whither he is falling, and set himself to serious seeking of God, cast down himself before him, abuse himself, cry for mercy, as for his life, there is yet hope in his case. God may here show an

example of what he can induce himself to do for a perishing wretch ! But,

IV. If with any that have lived under the gospel, their day is quite expired, and the things of their peace now for ever hid from their eyes, this is in itself a most deplorable case, and much lamented by our Lord Jesus himself. That the case is in itself most deplorable, who sees not ? A soul lost ! a creature capable of God ! upon its way to him ! near to the kingdom of God ! shipwrecked in the port ! O sinner, from how high a hope art thou fallen ! into what depths of misery and woe ! And that it was lamented by our Lord, is in the text. He beheld the city (very generally, we have reason to apprehend, inhabited by such wretched creatures), and wept over it. This was a very affectionate lamentation. We lament often, very heartily, many a sad case, for which we do not shed tears. But tears, such tears, falling from such eyes ! the issues of the purest and best governed passion that ever was, shewed the true greatness of the cause. Here could be no exorbitancy or unjust excess, nothing more than was proportionable to the occasion. There needs no other proof that this is a sad case, than that our Lord lamented it with tears, which that he did, we are plainly told, so that touching that, there is no place for doubt. All that is liable to question is, whether we are to conceive in him any like resentments of such cases, in his present glorified state ?

Indeed we cannot think heaven a place or state of sadness, or lamentation ; and must take heed of conceiving any thing there, especially on the throne of glory, unsuitable to the most perfect nature, and the most glorious state. We are not to imagine tears there, which in that happy region are wiped away from inferior eyes ; no grief, sorrow, or sighing, which are all fled away, and shall be no more : as there can be no other turbid passion of any kind. But when expressions that import anger, or grief, are used, even concerning God himself, we must sever in our conception every thing of imperfection, and ascribe every thing of real perfection. We are not to think such expressions signify nothing, that they have no meaning, or that nothing at all is to be attributed to him under them.

Nor are we again to think they signify the same thing with what we find in ourselves, and are wont to express by those names. In the divine nature, there may be real, and yet most serene, complacency and displacency, viz. that are unaccompanied with the least commotion, and import nothing of imperfection, but perfection rather, as it is a perfection to apprehend things suitably to what in themselves they are. The Holy Scriptures frequently speak of God as angry, and grieved for the sins of men, and their miseries which ensue therefrom. And a real aversion and dislike is signified thereby, and by many other expressions, which in us would signify vehement agitations of affection, that we are sure can have no place in him. We ought therefore in our own thoughts to ascribe to him that calm aversion of will, in reference to the sins and miseries of men in general ; and, in our own apprehensions, to remove to the utmost distance from him all such agitations of passion or affection, even though some expressions that occur, carry a great appearance thereof, should they be understood according to human measures, as they are human forms of speech. As, to instance in what is said by the glorious God himself, and very near in sense to what we have in the text, what can be more pathetic, than that lamenting wish, Psal. lxxxi. 13, O that my people had hearkened unto me, and Israel had walked in my ways !

But we must take heed lest, under the pretence that we cannot ascribe every thing to God that such expressions seem to import, we therefore ascribe nothing. We ascribe nothing, if we do not ascribe to a real unwillingness that men should sin on, and perish ; and consequently a real willingness that they should turn to him and live ; which so many plain texts assert. And therefore it is unavoidably imposed upon us, to believe that God is truly unwilling of some things, which he doth not think fit to interpose his omnipotency to hinder, and is truly willing of some things, which he doth not put forth his omnipotency to effect

That he most fitly makes this the ordinary course of his dispensations towards men, to govern them by laws, and promises, and threatenings (made most express to them that live under the gospel), to work upon their minds, their hope, and their fear ; affording them the ordinary assistances of supernatural light and influence, with which he requires them to comply, and which, upon their refusing to do so, he may most righteously withhold, and give them the victory to their own ruin ; though oftentimes he doth, from a sovereignty of grace, put forth that greater power upon others, equally negligent and obstinate, not to enforce, but effectually to incline, their wills, and gain a victory over them, to their salvation.

Nor is his will towards the rest altogether ineffectual, though it have not this effect. For whosoever thou art that livest under the gospel, though thou dost not know that God so wills thy conversion and salvation, as to effect it, whatsoever resistance thou now makest ; though thou art not sure he will finally overcome all thy resistance, and pluck thee as a firebrand out of the mouth of hell ; yet thou canst not say his good will towards thee hath been without any effect at all tending thereto. He hath often called upon thee in his gospel, to repent and turn to him through Christ ; he hath waited on thee with long patience, and given thee time and space of repentance ; he hath within that time been often at work with thy soul. Hath he not many times let in beams of light upon thee ? shewn thee the evil of thy ways ? convinced thee ? awakened thee ? half persuaded thee ? and thou never hadst reason to doubt, but that if thou hadst set thyself with serious diligence to work out thy own salvation, he would have wrought on, so as to have brought things to a blessed issue for thy soul.

Thou mightest discern his mind towards thee to be agreeable to his word, wherein he hath testified to thee he desired not the death of sinners, that he hath no pleasure in the death of him that dieth, or in the death of the wicked, but that he should turn and live ; exhorted thee, expostulated with thee, and others in thy condition, Turn ye, turn ye, why will ye die ? He hath told thee expressly thy stubbornness, and contending against him, did grieve him, and vex his Spirit ; that thy sin, wherein thou hast indulged thyself, hath been an abomination to him, that it was the abominable thing which his soul hated, that he was broken with the whorish heart of such as thou, and pressed therewith, as a cart that was full of sheaves.

Now such expressions as these, though they are borrowed from man, and must be understood suitably to God, though they do not signify the thing with him as they do in us, yet they do not signify nothing. As when hands and eyes are attributed to God, they do not signify as they do with us, yet they signify somewhat correspondent, as active and visive power : so these expressions, though they signify not, in God, such unquiet motions and passions, as they would in us, they do signify a mind and will, really, though with the most perfect calmness and tranquillity, set against sin, and the horrid consequences of it, which yet, for greater reasons than we can understand, he may not see fit to do all he can to prevent. And if we know not how to reconcile such a will in God, with some of our notions concerning the divine nature ; shall we, for what we have thought of him, deny what he hath so expressly said of himself, or pretend to understand his nature better than he himself doth ?*

And when we see from such express sayings in Scripture, reduced to a sense becoming God, how God's mind stands in reference to sinners, and their self-destroying ways, we may thence apprehend what temper of mind our Lord Jesus also bears towards them in the like case, even in his glorified state. For can you think there is a disagreement between him and the Father about these things ? And whereas we find our blessed Lord, in the days of his flesh, one while complaining men would not come to him that they might have life (John, v. 40), elsewhere grieved at the hardness of their hearts (Mark, iii. 5), and here scat-

* See the Appendix.

tering tears over sinning and perishing Jerusalem ; we cannot doubt but that the (innocent) perturbation, which his earthly state did admit, being severed, his mind is still the same, in reference to cases of the same nature; for can we think there is any disagreement between him and himself ? We cannot therefore doubt but that,

1. He distinctly comprehends the truth of any such case. He beholds from the throne of his glory above, all the treaties which are held and managed with sinners in his name, and what their deportments are therein. His eyes are as a flame of fire, wherewith he searches hearts, and trieth reins. He hath seen therefore, sinner, all along, every time an offer of grace hath been made to thee, and been rejected ; when thou hast slighted counsels and warnings that hath been given thee, exhortations and entreaties that have been pressed upon thee, for many years together, and how thou hast hardened thy heart against reproofs and threatenings, against promises and allurements ; and beholds the tendency of all this, what is like to come of it, and that, if thou persist, it will be bitterness in the end.

2. That he hath a real dislike of the sinfulness of thy course. It is not indifferent to him whether thou obeyest, or disobeyest the gospel ; whether thou turn and repent or no ; that he is truly displeased at thy trifling, sloth, negligence, impenitency, hardness of heart, stubborn obstinacy, and contempt of his grace, and takes real offence at them.

3. He hath real kind propensions towards thee, and is ready to receive thy returning soul, and effectually to mediate with the offended Majesty of heaven for thee, as long as there is any hope in thy case.

4. When he sees there is no hope, he pities thee, while thou seest it not, and dost not pity thyself. Pity and mercy above are not names only ; 'tis a great reality that is signified by them, and that hath place there, in far higher excellency and perfection, than it can with us poor mortals here below. Ours is but borrowed, and participated from that first fountain and original above. Thou dost not perish unlamented, even with the purest heavenly pity,

though thou hast made thy case incapable of remedy. As the well-tempered judge bewails the sad end of the malefactor, whom justice obliges him not to spare, or save.

And now let us consider what use is to be made of all this. And though nothing can be useful to the persons themselves, whom the Redeemer thus laments as lost, yet that he doth so, may be of great use to others.

Use. Which will partly concern those who do justly apprehend this is not their case ; and partly such as may be in great fear that it is.

I. For such as have reason to persuade themselves it is not their case. The best ground upon which any can confidently conclude this, is that they have in this their present day, through the grace of God, already effectually known the things of their peace, such, viz. as have sincerely, with all their hearts and souls, turned to God, taken him to be their God, and devoted themselves to him, to be his ; intrusting and subjecting themselves to the saving mercy and governing power of the Redeemer, according to the tenor of the gospel-covenant, from which they do not find their hearts to swerve or decline, but resolve, through divine assistance, to persevere herein all their days. Now for such as with whom things are already brought to that comfortable conclusion, I only say to them,

1. Rejoice and bless God that so it is. Christ your Redeemer rejoices with you, and over you ; you may collect it from his contrary resentment of their case who are past hope ; if he weep over them, he, no doubt, rejoices over you. There is joy in heaven concerning you. Angels rejoice, your glorious Redeemer presiding in the joyful concert. And should not you rejoice for yourselves ? Consider what a discrimination is made in your case ! To how many hath that gospel been a deadly savour, which hath proved a savour of life unto life to you ! How many have fallen on your right hand and your left, stumbling at the stone of offence, which to you is become the headstone of the corner, elect and precious ! Whence is this difference ? Did you never slight Christ ? never make light of offered mercy ?

was your mind never blind or vain ? was your heart never
hard or dead ? were the terms of peace and reconciliation
never rejected or disregarded by you ? How should you
admire victorious grace, that would never desist from striving with you till it had overcome ! You are the triumph
of the Redeemer's conquering love, who might have been
of his wrath and justice ! Endeavour your spirits may
taste, more and more, the sweetness of reconciliation, that
you may more abound in joy and praises. Is it not pleasant to you to be at peace with God ? to find that all con-
troversies are taken up between him and you ? that you
can now approach him, and his terrors not make you afraid ?
that you can enter into the secret of his presence, and solace
yourselves in his assured favour and love ? How should
you joy in God through Jesus Christ, by whom you have
received the atonement ! What have you now to fear ? If,
when you were enemies, you were reconciled by the death
of Christ, how much more, being reconciled, shall you be
saved by his life ? How great a thing have you to oppose
to all worldly troubles ! If God be for you, who can be
against you ? Think how mean it is for the friends of God,
the favourites of heaven, to be dismayed at the appearances
of danger that threaten them from the inhabitants of the
earth ! What if all the world were in a posture of hostility
against you, when the mighty Lord of all is your friend ?
Take heed of thinking meanly of his power and love ;
would any one diminish to himself, whom he takes for his
God ? All people will walk every one in the name of his
god ; why should not you much more in the name of yours,
glorying in him, and making your boast of him all the
day long ? O the reproach which is cast upon the glorious
name of the great God, by their diffidence and despondency,
who visibly stand in special relation to him, but fear the
impotent malice of mortal man more than they can trust
in his Almighty love ! If indeed you are justified by faith,
and have peace with God, it becomes you so to rejoice in
the hope of the glory of God, as also to glory in tribulation, and tell all the world that in his favour stands your

life, and that you care not who is displeased with you for
the things wherewith, you have reason to apprehend, he is
pleased.

2. Demean yourselves with that care, caution, and duti-
fulness that become a state of reconciliation. Bethink
yourselves that your present peace and friendship with God
is not original, and continued from thence, but hath been
interrupted and broken ; that your peace is not that of
constantly innocent persons. You stand not in this good
and happy state because you never offended, but as being
reconciled, and who therefore were once enemies. And
when you were brought to know, in that your day, which
you have enjoyed, the things belonging to your peace, you
were made to feel the smart and taste the bitterness of your
having been alienated, and enemies in your minds by
wicked works. When the terrors of God did beset you
round, and his arrows stuck fast in you, did you not then
find trouble and sorrow ? were you not in a fearful expectation of wrath and fiery indignation to consume and burn
you up as adversaries ? Would you not then have given
all the world for a peaceful word or look ? for any glimmering hope of peace ? How wary and afraid should you
be of a new breach ! How should you study acceptable
deportments, and to walk worthy of God unto all well-
pleasing ! How strictly careful should you be to keep
faith with him, and abide stedfast in his covenant ! How
concerned for his interest ! and in what agonies of spirit,
when you behold the eruptions of enmity against him from
any others ! not from any distrust, or fear of final prejudice
to his interest, but from the apprehension of the unrighteousness of the thing itself, and a dutiful love to his name,
throne, and government. How zealous should you be to
draw in others ! how fervent in your endeavours, within
your own sphere, and how large in your desires, extended
as far as the sphere of the universe, that every knee might
bow to him, and every tongue confess to him ! They
ought to be more deeply concerned for his righteous cause,
that remember they were once most unrighteously engaged

against it. And ought besides to be filled with compassion towards the souls of men, yet in an unreconciled state, as having known by the terrors of the Lord, and remembering the experienced dismalness and horror of that state, what it was to have divine wrath and justice armed against you with almighty power! And to have heard the thunder of such a voice, "I lift my hand to heaven, and swear I live for ever, if I whet my glittering sword, and my hand take hold on vengeance, I will recompense fury to mine adversaries, vengeance to mine enemies."— Do you not know what the case is like to be, when potsherds, that should strive but with the potsherds of the earth, venture to oppose themselves as antagonists to omnipotency? And when briars and thorns set themselves in battle-array against the consuming fire, how easily it can pass through, and devour, and burn them up together? And how much more fearful is their condition that know it not! but are ready to rush like the horse into the battle! Do you owe no duty, no pity to them that have the same nature with you, and with whom your case was once the same? If you do indeed know the things of your peace God-ward, so as to have made your peace, to have come to an agreement, and struck a covenant with him; you have now taken his side, are of his confederates; not as equals but subjects. You have sworn allegiance to him, and associated yourself with all them that have done so. There can hereupon be but one common interest to him and you. Hence therefore you are most strictly obliged to wish well to that interest, and promote it to your uttermost, in his own way, i. e. according to his openly avowed inclination and design, and the genuine constitution of that kingdom which he hath erected, and is intent to enlarge and extend further in the world. That, you do well know, is a kingdom of grace; for his natural kingdom already confines with the universe, and can have no enlargement, without enlarging the creation. Whosoever they are that contend against him, are not merely enemies, therefore, but rebels. And you see he aims to conquer them by love and goodness ; and therefore treats with them, and seeks to establish a kingdom over them, in and by a Mediator, who if he were not intent upon the same design, had never lamented the destruction of any of them, and wept over their ruin, as here you find. So, therefore, should you long for the conversion of souls, and enlargement of his kingdom this way, both out of loyalty to him, and compassion towards them.

II. For such as may be in great fear lest this prove to be their case. They are either such as may fear it, but do not ; or such as are deeply afflicted with this actual fear.

1. For the former sort, who are in too great danger of bringing themselves into this dreadful deplorate condition, but apprehend nothing of it. All that is to be said to them apart by themselves, is only to awaken them out of their drowsy, dangerous slumber and security ; and then they will be capable of being spoken to, together with the other sort. Let me therefore,

1. Demand of you ; do you believe there is a Lord over you, yea or no ? Use your thoughts, for, about matters that concern you less, you can think. Do you not apprehend you have an invisible Owner and Ruler, that rightfully claims to himself an interest in you, and a governing power over you ? How came you into being ? You know you made not yourselves. And if you yet look no higher than to progenitors of your own kind, mortal men, as you are ; how came they into being ? You have so much understanding about you, if you would use it, as to know they could none of them make themselves more than you, and that, therefore, human race must have had its beginning from some superior Maker. And did not he that made them make you and all things else ? Where are your arguments to prove it was otherwise, and that this world, and all the generations of men, took beginning of themselves, without a wise and mighty Creator ? Produce your strong reasons, upon which you will venture your souls, and all the possibilities of your being happy or miserable to eternity ! Will your imagination make you

safe ? and protect you against his wrath and justice, whose authority you will not own ? Can you, by it, uncreate your Creator, and nullify the eternal Being ? or have you any thing else, besides your own blind imagination, to make you confident, that all things came of nothing, without any maker ? But if you know not how to think this reasonable, and apprehend you must allow yourselves to owe your being to an Almighty Creator, let me,

2. Ask of you how you think your life is maintained ? Doth not he that made you live, keep you alive ? Whereas you have heard we all live, and move, and have our beings in him, doth it not seem most likely to you to be so ? Have you power of your own life ? Do you think you can live as long as you will ? At least do you not find you need the common helps of meat and drink, and air and clothing, for the support and comfort of your lives ? And are not all these his creatures as well as you ? And can you have them, whether he will or no ?

3. And how can you think that he that made and maintains you, hath no right to rule you ? If it were possible any one should as much depend upon you, would you not claim such power over him ? Can you suppose yourself to be under no obligation to please him, who hath done so much for you ? and to do his will, if you can any way know it ?

4. And can you pretend you have no means to know it ? That book that goes up and down under the name of his Word, can you disprove it to be his Word ? If such writings should now first come into the world, so sincere, so awful, so holy, so heavenly, bearing so expressly the divine image, avowing themselves to be from God, and the most wonderful works are wrought to prove them his word, the deaf made to hear, the blind to see, the dumb to speak, the sick healed, the dead raised, by a word only commanding it to be so, would you not confess this to be sufficient evidence that this revelation came from heaven ? And are you not sufficiently assured they are so confirmed ? Do you find in yourselves any inclination to cheat your

children, in any thing that concerns their wellbeing? Why should you more suspect your forefathers' design, to cheat you in the mere reporting falsely a matter of fact? Was not human nature the same, so many hundred years ago? Did ever the enemies of the Christian name, in the earlier days of Christianity, when it was but a novelty in the world, and as much hated, and endeavoured to be rooted out, as ever any profession was, deny such matters of fact? Have not some of the most spiteful of them confessed it? Did not Christians then willingly sacrifice their lives by multitudes, upon the assured truth of these things? Have they not been ever since most strictly careful to preserve these writings, and transmit them, as wherein the all of themselves and their posterity was contained? And where is now your new light? where are your latter discoveries, upon which, so many ages after, you are able to evict these writings of falsehood, or dare venture to disbelieve them?

5. But if you believe these writings to be divine, how expressly is it told you, in them, what the state of your case is God-ward, and what he requires of you! You may see you have displeased him, and how you are to please him, as hath been shewn before in this discourse. You know that you have lived in the world mindless and inobservant of him, not trusting, fearing, loving, or delighting in him, declining his acquaintance and converse; seeking your own pleasure, following your inclination, doing your own will; as if you were supreme, never minding to refer your actions to his precepts as your rule, or to his glory as your end. And from that word of his you may understand all this to be very displeasing to him. And that you can never please him by continuing this course, but by breaking it off, and returning to him as your Lord, and your God. That since your case did need a redeemer, and reconciler, and he hath provided and appointed one for you; you are to apply yourselves to him, to commit and subject your souls to him, to trust in his merits and blood, and submit to his authority and government. And,

6. Are you not continually called hereto by the gospel, under which you have lived all this while? so that you are in actual, continual rebellion against him all the while you comply not with this call; every breath you draw is rebellious breath. There is no moment wherein this lies not upon you, by every moment's addition to your time. And that patience of his which adds by moments to your life, and should lead you to repentance, is, while you repent not, perverted by you, only to the treasuring up of wrath against the day of wrath, and the revelation of his righteous judgment.

7. And do you not find, as his word also plainly tells you, a great averseness and disinclination in you to any such serious solemn applying yourself to him, and your Redeemer? Try your own hearts; do you not find them draw back and recoil? If you urge them, do they not still fly off? How loath are you to retire! and set yourselves to consider your case! and unto serious seeking of God in Christ! both from a reluctancy and indisposition to any such employment as this is itself, and from disaffection to that whereto it tends, the breaking off your former sinful course of life, and entering upon a better. And does not all this shew you the plain truth of what the word of God hath told you, that the Ethiopian may as soon change his skin, or the leopard his spots, as they do good who are accustomed to do evil (Jer. xiii. 23); that you have a heart that cannot repent (Rom. ii. 5), till God give you repentance to life (Acts, xi. 18), that you cannot come to Christ till the Father draw you, John, vi. 44. Do you not see your case then? that you must perish if you have not help from heaven, if God do not give you his grace, to overcome and cure the averseness and malignity of your nature? that things are likely thus to run on with you as they have from day to day, and from year to year; and you that are unwilling to take the course that is necessary for your salvation to-day, are likely to be as unwilling to-morrow, and so your lives consume in vanity, till you drop into perdition? But,

8. Dost thou not also know, sinner (what hath been so newly shewn thee from God's word), that, by thy being under the gospel, thou hast a day of grace? not only as offers of pardon and reconciliation are made to thee in it, but also as through it, converting, heart-renewing grace is to be expected, and may be had? that what is sufficient for the turning and changing of thy heart, is usually not given all at once, but as gentler insinuations (the injection of some good thoughts and desires) are complied with, more powerful influences may be hoped to follow? that therefore thou art concerned, upon any such thought cast into thy mind, of going now to seek God for the life of thy soul, to strive, thyself, against thy own disinclination? that if thou do not, but yield to it, and still defer, it may prove mortal to thee? For is it not plain to thee in itself, and from what hath been said, that this day hath its limits, and will come to an end? Dost thou not know thou art a mortal creature, that thy breath is in thy nostrils? Dost thou know how near thou art to the end of thy life? and how few breaths there may be for thee between this present moment and eternity? Dost thou not know thy day of grace may end before thy life? that thou mayst be cast far enough out of the sound of the gospel? and if thou shouldst carry any notices of it with thee, thou, who hast been so unapt to consider them, while they were daily pressed upon thee, wilt most probably be less apt when thou hearest of no such thing? that thou mayst live still under the gospel, and the Spirit of grace retire from thee, and never attempt thee more for thy former despiting of it? For what obligation hast thou upon that blessed Spirit? Or why shouldst thou think a Deity bound to attend upon thy triflings? And,

9. If yet all this move not: consider what it will be to die unreconciled to God! Thou hast been his enemy, he hath made thee gracious offers of peace, waited long upon thee, thou hast made light of all. The matter must at length end either in reconciliation or vengeance! The former is not acceptable to thee: art thou prepared for the

latter? canst thou sustain it? Is it not a fearful thing to fall into the hands of the living God? Thou wilt not do him right; he must then right himself upon thee. Dost thou think he cannot do it? canst thou doubt his power? Cast thine eyes about thee, behold the greatness (as far as thou canst) of this creation of his, whereof thou art a very little part. He that hath made that sun over thine head, and stretched out those spacious heavens, that hath furnished them with those innumerable bright stars, that governs all their motions, that hath hung this earth upon nothing, that made and sustains that great variety of creatures that inhabit it, can he not deal with thee, a worm? Can thine heart endure, or thine hands be strong, if he plead with thee? if he surround thee with his terrors, and set them in battle-array against thee? Hell and destruction are open before him, and without covering; how soon art thou cast in and ingulfed! Sit down, and consider whether thou be able, with *thy impotency*, to stand before him, that comes against thee with *almighty power!* Is it not better to sue in time for peace? But perhaps thou mayst say, " I begin now to fear it is too late, I have so long slighted the gospel, resisted the Holy Spirit of God, abused and baffled my own light and conscience, that I am afraid God will quite abandon me, and cast me off for ever." It is well if thou do indeed begin to fear. That fear gives hope. Thou art then capable of coming into their rank who are next to be spoken to, viz.

2. Such as feel themselves afflicted with the apprehension and dread of their having out-lived their day, and that the things of their peace are now irrecoverably hid from their eyes. I desire to counsel such faithfully, according to that light and guidance which the Gospel of our Lord affords us in reference to any such case.

1. Take heed of stifling that fear suddenly, but labour to improve it to some advantage, and then to cure and remove it by rational, evangelical means and methods. Do not, as thou lovest the life of thy soul, go about suddenly, or by undue means, to smother or extinguish it. 'Tis too

possible, when any such apprehension strikes into a man's mind, because 'tis a sharp or piercing thought, disturbs his quiet, gives him molestation, and some torture, to pluck out the dart too soon, and cast it away. Perhaps such a course is taken, as doth him unspeakably more mischief, than a thousand such thoughts would ever do. He diverts, it may be, to vain company, or to sensuality, talks or drinks away his trouble ; makes death his cure of pain, and to avoid the fear of hell, leaps into it. Is this indeed the wisest course ? Either thy apprehension is reasonable, or unreasonable. If it should prove a reasonable apprehension, as it is a terrible one, would the neglect of it become a reasonable creature, or mend thy case ? if it shall be found unreasonable, it may require time and some debate to discover it to be so ; whereby, when it is manifestly detected, with how much greater satisfaction is it laid aside ! Labour then to inquire rightly concerning this matter.

2. In this inquiry, consider diligently what the kind of that fear is that you find yourselves afflicted with. The fear that perplexes your heart, must some way correspond to the apprehension you have in your mind, touching your case. Consider what that is, and in what form it shews itself there. Doth it appear in the form of a peremptory judgment, a definitive sentence, which you have past within yourself concerning your case ; that your day is over, and you are a lost creature ? or only of a mere doubt, lest it should prove so ? The fear that corresponds to the former of these, makes you quite desperate, and obstinately resolute against any means for the bettering of your condition. The fear that answers to the latter apprehension, hath a mixture of hope in it, which admits of somewhat to be done for your relief, and will prompt thereunto. Labour to discern which of these is the present temper and posture of your spirit.

3. If you find it be the former, let no thought any longer dwell in your mind *under that form,* viz. as a definitive sentence concerning your state. You have nothing to do to pass such a judgment ; the tendency of it is dismal and

horrid, as you may, yourself, perceive. And your ground
for it is none at all. Your conscience within you is to do
the office of a judge ; but only of an under-judge, that is
to proceed strictly by rule, prescribed and set by the sovereign Lord and Arbiter of life and death : there is one
Lawgiver, who is able to save and to destroy. Nor is your
conscience, as an under-judge, to meddle at all, but in cases
within your cognizance. This about your final state is a
reserved, excepted case, belonging only to the supreme
tribunal, which you must take heed how you usurp. As
such a judgment tends to make you desperate, so there will
be high presumption in this despair. Dare you take upon
you to cancel and nullify to yourself the obligation of the
evangelical law ? and whereas that makes it your duty to
repent, and believe the gospel, to absolve yourselves from
this bond, and say, it is none of your duty, or make it
impossible to you to do it ? You have matter and cases
enough within the cognizance of your conscience, not only
the particular actions of your life, but your present state
also, whether you be as yet in a state of acceptance with
God, through Christ, yea or no. And here you have rules
set you to judge by. But concerning your final state, or
that you shall never be brought into a state of acceptance,
you have no rule by which you can make such a judgment;
and therefore this judgment belongs not to you. Look,
then, upon the matter of your final condition, as an exempt
case, reserved to the future judgment, and the present
determination whereof, against yourself, is without your
compass and line, and most unsuitable to the state of pro-
bation, wherein, you are to reckon, God continues you
here, with the rest of men in this world ; and therefore any
such judgment you should tear and reverse, and as such,
not permit to have any place with you.

4. Yet since, as hath been said, you are not quite to
reject or obliterate any apprehension or thought touching
this subject, make it your business to correct and reduce it
to that other form, *i. e.* let it only for the present remain
with you, as a doubt how your case now stands, and what

issue it may at length have. And see that your fear there-upon be answerable to your apprehension, so rectified. While as yet it is not evident you have made your peace with God upon his known terms, you are to consider God hath left your case a doubtful case, and you are to conceive of it accordingly; and are to entertain a fear concerning it, not as certainly hopeless, but as uncertain. And as yours is really a doubtful case, 'tis a most important one. It concerns your souls, and your eternal well-being, and is not therefore to be neglected, or trifled with. You do not know how God will deal with you : whether he will again afford you such help as he hath done, or whether ever he will effectually move your heart unto conversion and sal-vation. You therefore are to work out your salvation with fear and trembling, because (as was told you) he works, but of his own good pleasure. Your fear should not ex-ceed this state of your case, so as to exclude hope. It is of unspeakable concernment to you, that hope do inter-mingle with your fear. That will do much to mollify and soften your hearts, that after all the abuse of mercy, and imposing upon the patience of God, your neglects and slights of a bleeding Saviour, your resisting and grieving the Spirit of grace, he may yet, once for all, visit your for-lorn soul with his vital influence, and save you from going down to perdition ! How can your hearts but melt and break upon this apprehension ! And it is not a groundless one. He that " came not to call the righteous but sinners to repentance," will not fail to treat them well, whom he sees beginning to listen to his call, and entertaining the thoughts that most directly tend to bring them to a com-pliance with it. Your hope insinuating itself and mingling with your fear, is highly grateful to the God of all grace. He takes pleasure in them that fear him, and in them that hope in his mercy, Psal. cxlvii. 11.

5. But see to it also that your fear be not slight and momentary, and that it vanish not, while as yet it hath so great a work to do in you, viz. to engage you to accept God's own terms of peace and reconciliation, with all your

heart and soul. It is of continual use, even not only in order to conversion, but to the converted also. Can you think those mentioned words were spoken to none such, Phil. ii. 12, 13 ? or those, Heb. iv. 1 ? Let us therefore fear, lest a promise being left us of entering into his rest, any of you should seem to come short, &c. And do we not find a holy fear is to contribute all along to the whole of progressive sanctification ? 2 Cor. vii. 1. Having therefore these promises, dearly beloved, let us cleanse ourselves from all filthiness of the flesh and spirit, perfecting holiness in the fear of God. And that by it he preserves his own, that they never depart from him, Jer. xxxii. 40. Much more do you need it in your present case, while matters are yet in treaty between God and you. And as it should not exceed the true apprehension of your case, so neither should it come short of it.

6. You should therefore in order hereto aggravate to yourselves the just causes of your fear. Why are you afraid your day should be over, and the things of your peace be for ever hid from your eyes ? Is it not that you have sinned against much light, against many checks of your own consciences, against many very serious warnings and exhortations, many earnest importunate beseechings and entreaties you have had in the ministry of the gospel, many motions and strivings of the Spirit of God thereby ? Let your thoughts dwell upon these things. Think what it is for the great God, the Lord of glory, to have been slighted by a worm ! Doth not this deserve as ill things at the hands of God as you can fear ? 'Tis fit you should apprehend what your desert is, though perhaps mercy may interpose, and avert the deserved dreadful event. And if he have signified his displeasure towards you hereupon, by desisting for the present, and ceasing to strive with you as he hath formerly done ; if your heart be grown more cold, and dead, and hard, than sometime it was ; if you have been left so as to fall into grosser sin ; 'tis highly reasonable you should fear being finally forsaken of the blessed Spirit of God, and greatly fear it, but with an awful

fear that may awaken you most earnestly to endeavour his
return to you, not with a despairing fear, that will bind
you up from any further endeavour for your soul at all.

And if upon all this (by death or otherwise) such a
ministry be withdrawn from you as God did work by, in
some degree, upon you, and you find not in that kind,
what is so suitable to your state and case ; take heed lest
you be stupid under such a stroke.   Think what it imports
unto you, if God have, as it were, said concerning any
servant of his (as Ezek. iii. 26), I will make his tongue
cleave to the roof of his mouth, that he shall not be a
reprover to you any more !   Consider that God may by
this be making way that " wrath may come upon you to
the uttermost," and never let you have opportunity to
know more the things of your peace.   Perhaps you may
never meet with the man more, that shall speak so suitably to your condition, that shall so closely pursue
you through all the haunts, and subterfuges, and lurking-
holes, wherein your guilty convinced soul hath been wont
to hide itself, and falsely seek to heal its own wounds.
One of more value may be less apt, possibly, to profit you :
as a more polished key doth not therefore alike fit every lock.
And thy case may be such, that thou shalt never hear a
sermon or the voice of a preacher more.

7. And now in this case recollect yourselves, what sins
you have been formerly convinced of, under such a ministry,
and which you have persisted in notwithstanding.   Were
you never convinced of your neglecting God, and living as
without him in the world ? of your low esteem and disregard of Christ ? of your worldliness, your minding only
the things of this earth ? of your carnality, pride, self-
seeking, voluptuousness, your having been lovers of pleasures more than lovers of God ? of your unprofitableness in
your station ? wherein you ought to have lived more con-
formably to Christian rules and precepts, according to the
relations wherein God had set you ?   Were you never
convinced how very faulty governors you have been, or
members of families ? parents or masters, children or ser-

vants, &c. ? What will this come to at last, that convictions have hitherto signified and served for nothing but increase of guilt ?

8. Under all this weight and load of guilt, consider what you have to do for your souls ! Bethink yourselves : are you to sit down and yield yourselves to perish ? Consider, man, it is the business of thy soul, and of thine eternal state, that is now before thee. Thou hast the dreadful flaming gulf of everlasting horror and misery in view ; hast thou nothing left thee to do but to throw thyself into it ? Methinks thou shouldst sooner reconcile thy thoughts to any thing than that ; and that, if any thing at all be to be done for thine escape, thou shouldst rather set thyself about it, and do it. Thou art yet alive, not yet in hell, yet the patience of God spares thee, thou hast yet time to consider, thou hast the power to think yet left thee, and canst thou use it no other way than to think of perishing ? Think rather how not to perish. A great point is gained, if thou art but brought to say, " What shall I do to be saved ?" which doth imply thou dost both apprehend the distressedness of thy case, and art willing to do any thing that is to be done for thy relief. And if thou art brought to this, thy circumstances may perhaps be such, that thou canst only put this question to thyself, and art only thyself to answer it, without a living, present guide, which may therefore make such a help as this needful to thee. Possibly some irresistible providence may have so cast thy lot, that thou art only now to be thy own preacher ; though it sometime was otherwise with thee ; and things were said to thee most suitable to the condition of thy soul, which thou wouldst not then consider. It is yet pressed upon thee to consider now, with some design to direct thy thoughts, that they run not into useless and troublesome confusion only. And your subject being what course you are now to take, that you may escape eternal wrath and ruin, 'tis obvious to you to apprehend nothing is to be done against or without God, but with him, and by him. Your utmost consideration can but bring the matter to this short

point, that whereas you have highly offended the God that made you, incurred his wrath, and made him your enemy, either to resist, or treat and supplicate. That madness which would let you intend the *former*, is not capable of consideration at all. For, if you consider, will you contend with omnipotency, or fight with an all-devouring flame? And *as to the latter*, it is well for you, that it can be the matter of your consideration, that you have any encouragement to turn your thoughts that way. You might have enemies that, being provoked, and having you in their power, would never admit of a treaty, nor regard your supplications, but fall upon you with merciless fury, and leave you nothing to think of but perishing. Here it is not so with you. The merciful God hath graciously told you, fury is not so in him, but that (though if briars and thorns will set themselves in battle against him, he will easily pass through, and burn them up together, yet) if any will take hold of his strength, that they may make peace with him, they shall make peace with him, Isa. xxvii. 4, 5. You are to consider there is danger in your case, and there is hope, that your sin is not so little as to need no forgiveness, nor too great to be forgiven. Wherefore, whose case soever this is, since you may be forgiven, if you duly apply yourselves, and must be forgiven, or you are undone, my further advice to you is, and you may, as to this, advise yourself, having nothing else left you to do.

9. That you cast yourselves down before the mercy-seat of God, humble yourselves deeply at his footstool, turn to him with all your soul, implore his mercy through Christ, make a solemn covenant with him, taking him to be your God, and devoting yourself to him to be his, accepting his Son as your Lord and Saviour, and resigning your soul with submission and trust entirely to him, to be ruled and saved by him. That you are to do this, the case is plain, and even speaks itself; how you are to do it may need to be more particularly told you.

1. Take heed that what you do in this be not the mere effect of your present apprehended distress, but of the altered

judgment and inclination of your mind and heart. The apprehension of your distressed, dangerous condition, may be a useful means and inducement to engage you more seriously to listen and attend to the proposals made to you in the gospel. But if upon all this, it should be the sense of your heart that you would rather live still as without God in the world, and that you would never come to any such treaty or agreement with him; if mere necessity, and the fear of perishing, did not urge you to it, you are still but where you were. Therefore, though the feared danger was necessary to make you bethink yourself, and consider what God propounds to you ; that consideration ought to have that further effect upon you, to convince you of the equity and desirableness of the things themselves which he propounds, summarily, of your betaking yourselves to him as your sovereign Lord and supreme Good, to fear and love, obey and enjoy him, in Christ Jesus, and accordingly ought to incline your heart thereto.

2. You are to consider in your entering into this covenant with God in Christ, that it is not a transaction for the present only you are about, but for your whole life. This God is to be your God for ever and ever, your God and your guide even to the death, Psalm xlviii. 14. You are to live in his fear and love, in his service and communion, all your days, and must understand this to be the meaning and tenor of the covenant which you make with him.

3. And hence therefore, it is plain that your whole transaction in this matter must proceed from a new nature, and a new vital principle of grace and holiness in you. What you do herein will otherwise neither be sincere nor lasting. You can never embrace religion for itself, without this, nor continue on in a religious course. What you do only from a temporary pang of fear upon you, is but from a kind of force that is for the present upon you, and will come to nothing, as soon as the impression of that fear wears off. The religion which is true and durable, is not from a spirit of fear, but of love, power, and a sound mind, 2 Tim. i. 7. You must be a new creature, God's workmanship, created

in Christ Jesus unto good works—that you may walk in them. The life of the new creature stands in love to God, as its way and course afterwards is a course of walking with God. If your heart be not brought to love God, and delight in him, you are still but dead towards God, and you still remain alive unto sin, as before. Whereas, if you ever come to be a Christian indeed, you must be able truly to reckon yourself dead to sin, and alive to God through Jesus Christ, Rom. vi. 11. Whereupon in your making the mentioned covenant, you must yield yourself to God, as one that is alive from the dead, as 'tis verse 13 of the same chapter. A new nature and life in you, will make all that you do, in a way of duty (whether immediately towards God or man, the whole course of godliness, righteousness, and sobriety), easy and delightful to you. And because it is evident both from many plain scriptures, and your own and all men's experience, that you cannot be, yourselves, the authors of a new life and nature, you must therefore further, in entering into this covenant,

4. Most earnestly cry to God, and plead with him for his Spirit, by whom the vital unitive bond must be contracted between God and Christ and your souls. So this will be the covenant of life and peace. Lord! how generally do the Christians of our age deceive themselves with a self-sprung religion! Divine indeed in the institution, but merely human, in respect of the radication and exercise; in which respects also it must be divine or nothing. What, are we yet to learn that a divine power must work and form our religion in us, as well as divine authority direct and enjoin it? Do all such scriptures go for nothing that tell us, it is God that must create the new heart, and renew the right spirit in us; that he must turn us, if ever we be turned; that we can never come to Christ, except the Father draw us, &c.? Nor is there any cause of discouragement in this, if you consider what hath before been said in this discourse. Ask and you shall receive, seek and you shall find, knock and it shall be opened to you. Your heavenly Father will give his Spirit to them

that ask, more readily than parents do bread to their children, and not a stone. But what if you be put to ask often, and wait long, this doth but the more endear the gift, and shew the high value of it. You are to remember how often you have grieved, resisted, and vexed this Spirit, and that you have made God wait long upon you. What if the absolute sovereign Lord of all expect your attendance upon him? He waits to be gracious—and blessed are they that wait for him. Renew your applications to him. Lay from time to time that covenant before you, which yourselves must be wrought up unto a full entire closure with. And if it be not done at one time, try yet if it will another, and try again and again. Remember it is for your life, for your soul, for your all. But do not satisfy yourself with only such faint motions within thee, as may only be the effects of thy own spirit, of thy dark, dull, listless, sluggish, dead, hard heart, at least not of the efficacious regenerating influence of the divine Spirit. Didst thou never hear what mighty workings there have been in others, when God hath been transforming and renewing them, and drawing them into living union with his Son, and himself through him? What an amazing penetrating light hath struck into their hearts! as 2 Cor. iv. 6. Such as when he was making the world, enlightened the chaos. Such as hath made them see things that concerned them as they truly were, and with their own proper face, God, and Christ, and themselves, sin and duty, heaven and hell, in their own true appearances! How effectually they have been awakened! how the terrors of the Almighty have beset and seized their souls! what agonies and pangs they have felt in themselves, when the voice of God hath said to them, Awake, thou that sleepest, and arise from the dead, and Christ shall give thee light! Eph. v. 14. How he hath brought them down at his feet, thrown them into the dust, broken them, melted them, made them abase themselves, loathe and abhor themselves, filled them with sorrow, shame, confusion, and with indignation towards their own guilty souls, habituated them to a severity against themselves, unto the most sharp, and yet most unforced self-accusations, self-judging, and self-condemnation ; so as even to make them lay claim to hell, and confess the portion of devils belonged to them, as their own most deserved portion. And if now their eyes have been directed towards a Redeemer, and any glimmering of hope hath appeared to them ; if now they are taught to understand God saying to them, Sinner, art thou yet willing to be reconciled, and accept a Saviour ? O the transport into which it puts them ! this is life from the dead ! What, is there hope for such a lost wretch as I ? How tasteful now is that melting invitation ! how pleasant an intimation doth it carry with it ! Come unto me all ye that are weary and heavy laden, and I will give you rest, &c. If the Lord of heaven and earth do now look down from the throne of glory, and say, " What ! sinner, wilt thou despise my favour and pardon, my Son, thy mighty merciful Redeemer, my grace and Spirit still ?—What can be the return of the poor abashed wretch, overawed by the glory of the divine Majesty, stung with compunction, overcome with the intimation of kindness and love ? I have heard of thee, O God, by the hearing of the ear, now mine eye seeth thee ; wherefore I abhor myself, and repent in dust and ashes. So inwardly is the truth of that word now felt, That thou mayest remember and be confounded, and never open thy mouth any more because of thy shame, when I am pacified towards thee, for all that thou hast done, saith the Lord God, Ezek. xvi. 63. But, sinner, wilt thou make a covenant with me and my Christ ? wilt thou take me for thy God, and him for thy Redeemer and Lord ? And may I, Lord ? yet, may I ? O admirable grace ! wonderful sparing mercy ! that I was not thrown into hell at my first refusal ! Yea, Lord, with all my heart and soul, I renounce the vanities of an empty cheating world, and all the pleasures of sin. In thy favour stands my life. Whom have I in heaven but thee ? whom on earth do I desire besides thee ? And O, thou blessed Jesus, thou Prince of the kings of the earth, who hast loved me, and washed me from my sins in thy blood, and whom the eternal God hath exalted to be a Prince and a Saviour, to give repentance and remission of sins, I fall before thee, my Lord and my God; I here willingly tender my homage at the footstool of thy throne. I take thee for the Lord of my life. I absolutely surrender and resign myself to thee. Thy love constrains me henceforth no more to live to myself, but to thee who diedst for me, and didst rise again. And I subject and yield myself to thy blessed light and power, O Holy Spirit of grace, to be more and more illuminated, sanctified, and prepared for every good word and work in this world, and for an inheritance among them that are sanctified in the other. Sinner, never give thy soul leave to be at rest till thou find it brought to some such transaction with God (the Father, Son, and Spirit) as this ; so as that thou canst truly say, and dost feel thy heart is in it. Be not weary or impatient of waiting and striving, till thou canst say, this is now the very sense of thy soul. Such things have been done in the world (but O how seldom of latter days !) so God hath wrought with men to save them from going down to the pit, having found a ransom for them. And why may he not yet be expected to do so ? He hath smitten rocks ere now, and made the waters gush out ; nor is his hand shortened, nor his ear heavy. Thy danger is not, sinner, that he will be inexorable, but lest thou shouldst. He will be entreated, if thou wouldst be prevailed with to entreat his favour with thy whole heart.

And that thou mayst, and not throw away thy soul, and so great a hope, through mere sloth, and loathness to be at some pains for thy life ; let the text, which hath been thy *directory* about the things that belong to thy peace, be also thy *motive*, as it gives thee to behold the Son of God weeping over such as would not know those things. Shall not the Redeemer's tears move thee ? O hard heart ! Consider what these tears import to this purpose.

1. They signify the real depth and greatness of the misery into which thou art falling. They drop from an

intellectual and most comprehensive eye, that sees far, and pierces deep into things, hath a wide and large prospect ; takes the comfort of that forlorn state into which unreconcilable sinners are hastening, in all the horror of it. The Son of God did not weep vain and causeless tears, or for a light matter ; nor did he for himself either spend his own, or desire the profusion of others' tears. Weep not for ·me, O daughters of Jerusalem, &c. He knows the value of souls, the weight of guilt, and how low it will press and sink them ; the severity of God's justice, and the power of his anger, and what the fearful effects of them will be, when they finally fall. If thou understandest not these things thyself, believe him that did, at least believe his tears.

2. They signify the sincerity of his love and pity, the truth and tenderness of his compassion. Canst thou think his deceitful tears ? his, who never knew guile ? was this like the rest of his course ? And remember that he who shed tears, did, from the same fountain of love and mercy, shed blood too ! Was that also done to deceive ? Thou makest thyself some very considerable thing indeed, if thou thinkest the Son of God counted it worth his while to weep, and bleed, and die, to deceive thee into a false esteem of him and his love. But if it be the greatest madness imaginable to entertain any such thought, but that his tears were sincere and inartificial, the natural genuine expressions of undissembled benignity and pity, thou art then to consider what love and compassion thou art now sinning against ; what bowels thou spurnest ; and that if thou perishest, 'tis under such guilt as the devils themselves are not liable to, who never had a Redeemer bleeding for them, nor, that we ever find, weeping over them.

3. They shew the remedilessness of thy case, if thou persist in impenitency and unbelief till the things of thy peace be quite hid from thine eyes. These tears will then be the last issues of (even defeated) love, of love that is frustrated of its kind design. Thou mayst perceive in

these tears the steady unalterable laws of heaven, the inflexibleness of the divine justice, that holds thee in adamantine bonds, and hath sealed thee up, if thou prove incurably obstinate and impenitent, unto perdition ; so that even the Redeemer himself, he that is mighty to save, cannot at length save thee, but only weep over thee, drop tears into thy flame, which assuage it not ; but (though they have another design, even to express true compassion) do yet unavoidably heighten and increase the fervour of it, and will do so to all eternity. He even tells thee, sinner, " Thou hast despised my blood, thou shalt yet have my tears." That would have saved thee, these do only lament thee lost.

But the tears wept over others, as lost and past hope, why should they not yet melt thee, while as yet there is hope in thy case ? If thou be effectually melted in thy very soul, and looking to him whom thou hast pierced, dost truly mourn over him, thou mayst assure thyself the prospect his weeping eye had of lost souls, did not include thee. His weeping over thee would argue thy case forlorn and hopeless : thy mourning over him will make it safe and happy. That it may be so, consider further, that,

4. They signify how very intent he is to save souls, and how gladly he would save thine, if yet thou wilt accept of mercy while it may be had. For if he weep over them that will not be saved, from the same love that is the spring of these tears, would saving mercies proceed to those that are become willing to receive them. And that love that wept over them that were lost, how will it glory in them that are saved ? There his love is disappointed and vexed, crossed in its gracious intendment ; but here having compassed it, how will he joy over thee with singing, and rest in his love ! And thou also, instead of being involved in a like ruin with the unreconciled sinners of the old Jerusalem, shalt be enrolled among the glorious citizens of the new, and triumph together with them in eternal glory.

APPENDIX

BECAUSE some things, not fit to be wholly omitted, were as little fit to come into the body of a practical discourse, 'twas thought requisite to subjoin here the following additions, that will severally have reference to distinct parts of the foregoing discourse.

As to what was said of the unreasonableness and ill consequence of admitting it—to be any man's duty to believe himself utterly rejected, and forsaken of God, inasmuch as it would make that his duty which were repugnant to his felicity :—this is to be evinced by a consideration, which also, even apart by itself, were not without its own great weight, viz. that such a belief were inconsistent with his former stated and known duty ; it were therefore inconsistent with his felicity, inasmuch as it would make that duty impossible to be performed, which before, was by constitution of the evangelical law, made necessary to it, viz. repentance towards God, and faith in our Lord Jesus Christ. The hope of acceptance is so necessary to both these, that the belief of a man's being finally rejected, or that he shall never be accepted, cannot but make them both impossible, equally impossible as if he were actually in hell, as much impossible to him as to the devils themselves. Nor is this impossibility merely from a moral impotency, or that objuration of heart which were confessedly vicious, and his great sin, but from the natural influence of that belief of his being for ever rejected, which (upon the mentioned supposition) were his duty. Besides, inasmuch as it is the known duty of a sinner under the gospel, to turn to God through Christ, and it is also declared in the same gospel (sufficiently to make it the common matter of faith to Christians) that none can of themselves turn to God, and believe in his Son, without the help of special efficacious grace ; it must hereupon be a man's duty also to pray for that grace which may enable him hereto. How deep in wickedness was Simon Magus, even in the gall of bitterness and bond of iniquity, when yet Peter calls him to repentance, and puts him upon praying for forgiveness (which must imply also his praying for the grace to repent) ; but how can a man pray for that, which, at the same time, he believes shall not be given him ? yea, and which is harder, and more unaccountable, how can he stand obliged in duty, to pray for that which, at the same time, he stands obliged in duty to believe he shall not obtain ? How can these two contrary obligations lie upon a man at the same time ? or is he to look upon the former as ceased ? should he reckon the gospel as to him repealed ? or his impenitency and infidelity, even when they are at the highest, no sins ?

I know 'tis obvious to object, as to all this, the case of the unpardonable blasphemy against the Holy Ghost ; which will be supposed to be stated and determined in the sacred Scriptures ; and being so, the person that hath committed it, may equally be thought obliged (by a mixed assent, partly of faith to what is written, partly of self-knowledge, which he ought to have of his own acts and state) to conclude himself guilty of it ; whereupon all the former inconvenience and difficulty will be liable to be urged as above. But even as to this also, I see not but it may fitly enough be said, that though the general nature of that sin be stated, and sufficiently determined in *thesi*, yet that God hath not left it determinable in *hypothesi*, by any particular person, that he hath committed it. For admit that it generally lies in imputing to the devil those works of the Holy Ghost, by which the truth of Christianity was to be demonstrated, I yet see not how any man can apply this to his own particular case, so as justly and

certainly to conclude himself guilty of it.   I take it for
granted none will ever take the notion of blasphemy in
that strictness, but that a man may possibly be guilty of
this sin as well in thought as by speech.   I also doubt not
but it will be acknowledged on all hands, that prejudice and
malice against Christianity must have a great ingrediency
into this sin ; not such malice as whereby, knowing it to
be the true religion, a man hates and detests it as such
(which would suppose these Pharisees, whom our Saviour
charges with it, or cautions against it, to have been, at that
time, in their judgments and consciences, Christians), but
such malignity, and strong prejudice, as darkens and
obstructs his mind, that he judges it not to be true, against
the highest evidence of its being.   It will also be acknowledged, that some enmity and disaffection to true
religion is common to all men ; more especially in their
unregeneracy, and unconverted state.

Now let it be supposed that some person or other, of a
very unwarrantably sceptical genius, had opportunity to
know certainly the matter of fact, touching the miraculous
works wrought by our Saviour, and understood withal
somewhat generally of the doctrine which he taught ; and
that he sets himself, as a philosopher, to consider the case.
Suppose that, partly through prejudice against the holy
design of Christianity, whereof there is some degree in all,
and partly through shortness of discourse, not having
thoroughly considered the matter ; he thinks it possible
that some demon or other, with design, under a specious
pretence, to impose upon or amuse the credulous vulgar,
may have done all those strange things ; suppose his judgment should for the present more incline this way : what
if, thinking this to be the case in the instance of Appollonius
Tyanæus, he hath not yet, upon a slighter view, discerned
enough to distinguish them, but thinks alike of both cases :
yea, and suppose he have spoken his sentiments to some
or other : perhaps upon further inquiry and search, he
might see cause to alter his judgment; and now, setting
himself to inquire more narrowly, he perceives the unex-

ceptionable excellent scope and tendency of our Saviour's doctrine and precepts, considers the simplicity and purity of his life, contemplates further the awful greatness of his mighty works : but amidst these his deliberations, he finds among the rest of Christian constitutions this severe one, Matt. xii. 31, 32, and begins to fear lest, supposing the truth of this excellent religion, he have precluded himself of all the advantages of it by that former judgment of his. What is he to do in this case ? what were he to be advised unto ? What, to pass judgment upon himself, and his case, as desperate ? or not rather to humble himself before the God of heaven, ask pardon for his injurious rash judgment, and supplicate for mercy, and for further illumination, in the mystery of God, of the Father, and of Christ ? Which course, that it may have a blessed issue with him, who dare venture to deny or doubt ? And what have we to say hereupon, but that in great wisdom and mercy, our Saviour hath only told us there is such a sin, and what the general nature of it is, or whereabouts it lies, but the judgment of particular cases wherein, or of the very pitch and degree of malignity wherewith, it is committed, he hath reserved to himself ; intending further to strive with persons by his Spirit, while he judges them yet within the reach of mercy, or withhold it, when he sees any to have arrived to that culminating pitch of malignity and obstinacy, wherein he shall judge this sin specially to consist ? And what inconvenience is it to suppose he hath left this matter, touching the degree, humanly undeterminable ? The knowledge of it can do them who have committed it no good : and probably they have by it so blinded and stupified their own souls, as to have made themselves very little capable of apprehending that they have committed it, or of considering whether they have or no. But they are sunk into a deep abyss of darkness and death, so as that such knowledge may be as little possible, as it would be useful to them. All their faculties of intellection, consideration, and self-reflection, being (as to any such exercise) bound up in a stupefying dead sleep.

And to what purpose should they have a rule by which to determine a case, who—1. Can receive no benefit by the determination, and—2. Who are supposed when they use it, to have no faculty sufficiently apt to make this sad (but true) judgment of their case by it? But for them who have not committed it, and who are consequently yet capable of benefit by what should be made known about it, there is, therefore, enough made known for their real use and benefit. It will,

1. Be of real use to many such, to know their danger of running into it. And it is sufficient to that purpose, that they are plainly told wherein the general nature of it consists, or whereabouts it lies; without shewing them the very point that hath certain death in it; or letting them know just how near they may approach it, without being sure to perish, when there is danger enough in every step they take toward it. As if there were some horrid desert, into any part whereof no man hath any business to come, but in some part whereof there is a dreadful gulf, whence arises a *contagious halitus*, which, if he come within the verge of it, will be certainly poisonous and mortal to him. What need is there that any man should know just how near he may come, without being sure to die for it? He is concerned to keep himself at a cautious awful distance.

2. It may be of great use to others, that are afflicted with very torturing fears lest they have committed it, to know that they have not. And they have enough also to satisfy them in the case. For their very fear itself, with its usual concomitants in such afflicted minds, is an argument to them that they have not. While they find in themselves any value of divine favour, any dread of his wrath, any disposition to consider the state of their souls, with any thought or design of turning to God, and making their peace; they have reason to conclude God hath hitherto kept them out of that fearful gulf; and is yet in the way, and in treaty with them. For since we are not sufficient to think any thing (that good is) of ourselves, it is much more reasonable to ascribe any such thought or agitation

of spirit that have this design to him, than to ourselves, and to account that he is yet at work with us (at least in the way of common grace), though when our thoughts drive towards a conclusion against ourselves, that we have committed that sin, and towards despair thereupon, we are to apprehend a mixture of temptation in them, which we are concerned earnestly to watch and pray against. And yet even such temptation is an argument of such a one's not having committed that sin. For such as the devil may apprehend more likely to have committed it (and 'tis not to be thought he can be sure who have), he will be less apt to trouble with such thoughts, not knowing what the issue of that unquietness may prove, and apprehending it may occasion their escaping quite out of his snare. And I do conceive this to be a safer method, of satisfying such as are perplexed with this fear in our days, than to be positive in stating that sin so, or limiting it to such circumstances, as shall make it impossible to be committed in this age of the world. For let it be seriously considered, whether it be altogether an unsupposable thing, that, with some in our days, there may be an equivalency, in point of light and evidence of the truth of Christianity, unto what these Jews had, whom our Saviour warns of the danger of this sin, at that time when he so warned them ; his warning and cautioning them about it, implies that he judged them at least in a possibility, at that time, of incurring the guilt of it ; if the text Matt. xii. do not also imply that he reckoned them, then, actually to have committed it. For it is said, ver. 25, he knew their thoughts, *i. e.* considered the temper of their minds, and thereupon said to them what follows concerning it. Let us consider wherein their advantage towards their being ascertained of the truth of the Christian religion, was greater than we now can have. It was, chiefly, in this respect greater, that they had a nearer and more immediate knowledge of the matter of fact, wherein that evidence which our Saviour refers to did consist. A more immediate way of knowing it they had ; the most immediate the person·

whom he warns (or charges) seem not to have had ; for
those Pharisees, it is said, heard of the cure of the demo-
niac, not that they saw it. They took it upon the (no
doubt sufficiently credible) report of others. Now let it
be further considered, what we have to balance this one
single advantage. We have, to intelligent considering persons, rationally sufficient evidence of the same matter of
fact. But how great things, that have since followed, have
we the sufficiently certain knowledge of besides, beyond
what they had in view, at that time ! As the wonderful
death of our Lord, exactly according to prediction, in many
respects, together with all the unforetold amazing circumstances that attended it ! his more wonderful resurrection,
upon which so great a stress is laid for demonstrating the
truth of the religion he taught : the destruction of Jerusalem, as he foretold, and the shattered condition of the
Jewish nation, as was also foretold, ever since : the strange
success of the gospel in the first, and some following ages,
by so unlikely means, against the greatest opposition
imaginable, both of Jews and pagans. Not to insist on the
apostasy foretold, in the Christian church, with many more
things that might be mentioned. Let it be considered
whether the want of so immediate way of knowing some
or these things be not abundantly compensated by the
greatness of the other things that are however sufficiently
known. And if such as have wit and leisure to consider
these things in our days, are often pressed to consider them,
have them frequently represented, and laid before their
eyes, if such, I say, have in view as great evidence, upon
the whole, of the truth of Christianity, as these Pharisees
had ; it is then further to be considered, whether it be not
possible that some such may equal the Jewish malice,
against the holy design of our religion. To which I only
say, the Lord grant that none may. But if there be really
cause to apprehend such a danger, some other way should
be thought of to cure the trouble of some, than by the
danger and (too probable) ruin of others. However, none
should themselves make their own case incurable, by con-

cluding that they have sinned that sin, or by believing they are, otherwise, forsaken and rejected of God ; so as that he will never more assist their endeavour to repent, and turn to him through the Mediator.

If it be inquired here, since, as hath been shewn, some may be quite forsaken of God, while yet they live in the world ; ought such to believe then they are not forsaken, and so believe an untruth that they may make it true, or try if they can better their condition by it ? I answer, nor that neither. For that God will further assist an obstinate sinner, that hath long resisted his Spirit, and despised his mercy, is no matter of promise to him, and so no matter of faith. When he doth conquer, at length, any such, 'tis of mere unpromised favour (as was also shewn) ; whereof therefore he gives others no ground to despair ; and for which they are deeply concerned, with great earnestness, to supplicate. But if it be said, how can they pray for that whereof they have no promise ? and can have no faith, since what is not of faith is sin, Rom. xiv. 23. I answer, that passage of Scripture would, in this case, be much misapplied. It speaks not of faith concerning the certainty of any event to be expected, but the lawfulness of a work to be done, and of doubting, not concerning the event, but my own act. Can any man in his wits doubt concerning his own act in this case ? whether it be better to pray for the grace of God to save him, than slight it and perish ? Nor are they without very encouraging promises concerning the event, that God will be a rewarder of them that diligently seek him, Heb. xi. 6. And that whosoever shall call upon the name of the Lord shall be saved, Rom. x. 13, which promises, 'tis true, the context of both shews, do speak of believing prayer. They are to faith, not of it, and import, that God will reward and save the believer : not that he will give faith to the obstinate, contemptuous unbeliever. If he do this, 'tis (as was said) of unpromised bounty. But though they are not promises to give faith, they should induce it ; and incline sinners to cast themselves down before the throne of so gracious a God, and seek grace to help them in their need, in confidence that he will never reject penitent believing prayer. They, indeed, that for their former wilful sinning are utterly forsaken of God, will not thus apply themselves; but our question is not what they will do, but what they should. Because they would not, therefore they were forsaken, and because they yet will not, they are still and finally forsaken. Their refusal proceeds not from any discouragement God hath given them, but from the malignity of their own hearts. God hath not repealed his gospel towards them. The connexion continues firm between the perceptive and promissory parts of it. Their infidelity is not become their duty, but remains their heinous sin, and the more deeply heinous by how much their own malignity holds them more strongly in it.

Unto what also is discoursed concerning anger and grief (or other passions), ascribed to God, it will not be unfit here to add, that unless they be allowed to signify real aversion of will, no account is to be given what reality in him they can signify at all. For to say (what some do seem to satisfy themselves with) that they are to be understood *secundum effectum*, not *secundum affectum*, though true as to the negative part, is, as to the affirmative, very defective and short; for the effects of anger and grief, upon which those names are put, when spoken of God, are not themselves in him, but in us. But we are still at a loss what they signify in him. Such effects must have some cause. And if they be effects which he works, they must have some cause in himself that is before them, and productive of them. This account leaves us to seek what that cause is, that is signified by these names. That it cannot be any passion, as the same names are wont to signify with us, is out of question. Nor indeed do those names primarily, and most properly, signify passion in ourselves. The passion is consequently only by reason of that inferior nature in us, which is susceptible of it. But the aversion of our mind and will is before it, and, in another subject, very separable from it, and possible to be without it. In the blessed God we cannot understand any thing less is signified than real displeasure at the things whereat he is said to be angry or grieved.

Our shallow reason indeed is apt to suggest in these matters, Why is not that prevented that is so displeasing? And it would be said with equal reason in reference to all sin permitted to be in the world, Why was it not prevented? And what is to be said to this? Shall it be said that sin doth not displease God? that he hath no will against sin? it is not repugnant to his will? Yes; it is to his revealed will, to his law. But is that an untrue revelation? His law is not his will itself, but the *signum*, the discovery of his will. Now, is it an insignificant sign? a sign that signifies nothing? or to which there belong no correspondent *significatum? nothing that is signified by it?* Is that which is signified (for sure no one will say it signifies nothing) his real will, yea or no? who can deny it? That will, then (and a most calm, sedate, impassionate will it must be understood to be), sin, and consequently the consequent miseries of his creatures, are repugnant unto. And what will is that? 'Tis not a peremptory will concerning the event, for the event falls out otherwise; which were, upon that supposition, impossible; for who hath resisted his will? as was truly intimated by the personated questionist (Rom. ix. 19), but impertinently, when God's will of another (not a contrary) kind, *i. e.* concerning another object, was in the same breath referred unto, Why doth he yet find fault? 'Tis not the will of the event that is the measure of faultiness; for then there could not have been sin in the world, nor consequently misery, which only, by the Creator's pleasure, stands connected with it. For nothing could fall out against that irresistible will. The objector then destroys his own objection, so absurdly, and so manifestly, as not to deserve any other reply than that which he meets with. Nay, but who art thou, O man, that repliest against God?

And what is the other object about which the divine will is also conversant? Matter of duty, and what stands in connexion with it, not abstractly and separately, but as it is so connected, our felicity. This is objectively another will, as we justly distinguish divine acts, that respect the creature, by their indifferent objects. Against this will falls out all the sin and misery in the world.

All this seems plain and clear, but is not enough. For it may be further said, When God wills this or that to be my duty, doth he not will this event, viz. my doing it? otherwise wherein is his will withstood, or not fulfilled, in my not doing it? He willed this to be my duty, and it is so. I do not nor can hinder it from being so, yet I do it not, and that he willed not. If all that his will meant was that this should be my duty, but my doing it was not intended; his will is entirely accomplished, it hath its full effect, in that such things are constituted, and do remain my duty, upon his signification of this his will, my not doing it not being within the compass of the object, or the thing willed.

If it be said, he willed my doing it, i. e. that I should do it, not that I shall, the same answer will recur, viz. that his will hath still its full effect, this effect still remaining, that I should do it, but that I shall he willed not.

It may be said, I do plainly go against his will however; for his will was that I should do so or so, and I do not what he willed I should. 'Tis true, I go herein against his will, if he willed not only my obligation, but my action according to it. And indeed it seems altogether unreasonable, and unintelligible, that he should will to oblige me to that, which he doth not will me to do.

Therefore it seems out of question, that the holy God doth constantly and perpetually, in a true sense, will universal obedience, and the consequent felicity of all his creatures capable thereof; i. e. he doth will it with simple complacency, as what were highly grateful to him, simply considered by itself. Who can doubt, but that purity, holiness, blessedness, wheresoever they were to be beheld among his creatures, would be a pleasing and delightful spectacle to him, being most agreeable to the perfect

excellency, purity, and benignity of his own nature, and
that their deformity and misery must be consequently un-
pleasing ?   But he doth not efficaciously will every thing
that he truly wills.   He never willed the obedience of all
his intelligent creatures so, as effectually to make them
all obey, nor their happiness, so as to make them all be
happy, as the event shews.   Nothing can be more certain,
than that he did not so will these things ; for then nothing
could have fallen out to the contrary, as we see much hath.
Nor is it at all unworthy the love and goodness of his
nature not so to have willed, with that effective will, the
universal fulness, sinlessness, and felicity of all his intelligent creatures.   The divine nature comprehends all excel-
lencies in itself, and is not to be limited to that one only
of benignity, or an aptness to acts of beneficence.   For
then it were not infinite, not absolutely perfect, and so not
divine.   All the acts of his will must be consequently
conformable and agreeable to the most perfect wisdom.   He
doth all things according to the counsel of his will.   He
wills, 'tis true, the rectitude of our actions, and what would
be consequent thereto, but he first, and more principally,
wills the rectitude of his own. And he wills not only not to do
an unrighteous, but not an inept, or unfit thing.   We find he
did not think it fit efficaciously to provide concerning all
men, that they should be made obedient and happy, as he
hath concerning some.   That in the general he makes a
difference, is to be attributed to his wisdom, *i. e.* his wisdom
hath in the general made this determination, not to deal
with all alike, and so we find it ascribed to his wisdom that
he doth make a difference : and in what a transport is the
holy apostle in the contemplation and celebration of it
upon this account ! Rom. xi. 33. "O the depth of the
riches both of the wisdom and knowledge of God ! how
unsearchable are his judgments, and his ways past finding
out !" But now when, in particular, he comes to make this
difference between one person and another, there being no
reason in the object to determine him this way, more than
that, his designing some for the objects of special favour,

and waving others (as to such special favour), when all were in themselves alike ; in that case wisdom hath not so proper an exercise, but it is the work of free, unobliged sovereignty here to make the choice. " Having predestinated us unto the adoption of children, by Jesus Christ, to himself, according to the good pleasure of his will," Ephes. i. 5.

Yet in the mean time, while God doth not efficaciously will all men's obedience introductive of their happiness, doth it follow he wills it not really at all ? To say he wills it efficaciously, were to contradict experience, and his word ; to say he wills it not really, were equally to contradict his word. He doth will it, but not primarily, and as the more principal object of his will, so as to effect it notwithstanding whatsoever unfitness he apprehends in it, viz. that he so overpower all, as to make them obedient and happy. He really wills it, but hath greater reasons than this or that man's salvation, why he effects it not. And this argues no imperfection in the divine will, but the perfection of it, that he wills things agreeably to the reasonableness and fitness of them.

Other Solid Ground Titles